MYSTERIES OF
THE OLD TESTAMENT

From Joseph and Asenath
to the Prophet Malachi
&
The Ark of the Covenant and
The Mystery of the Promise

A. C. Emmerick

MYSTERIES OF THE OLD TESTAMENT

From Joseph and Asenath to the Prophet Malachi
&
The Ark of the Covenant and The Mystery of the Promise

From the Visions of
ANNE CATHERINE EMMERICH

Selected, Edited & Arranged
With Extensive New Translations from
the Original Notes of Clemens Brentano by
JAMES R. WETMORE

Volume 2 of 12
of the Series: *New Light on the*
Visions of Anne Catherine Emmerich

(With 24 Illustrations)

Angelico Press

First published in the USA
by Angelico Press 2018
Revised Text, New Text, Translations,
and Layout © James R. Wetmore 2018

For information, address:
Angelico Press
169 Monitor St.
Brooklyn, NY 11222
angelicopress.com

ISBN 978-1-62138-363-5 (pbk)
ISBN 978-1-62138-364-2 (cloth)
ISBN 978-1-62138-365-9 (ebook)

Cover Image:
J. James Tissot (French, 1836–1902)
Moses and the Ten Commandments
Cover Design: Michael Schrauzer

CONTENTS

Preface

ANNE Catherine Emmerich was born on September 8, 1774, at Flamske, near Coesfeld, Germany. From early childhood she was blessed with the gift of spiritual sight and lived almost constantly in inner vision of scenes of the Old and New Testaments. As a child, her visions were mostly of pre-Christian events, but these grew less frequent with the passing years, and by the time she had become, at twenty-nine, an Augustinian nun at the Order's convent in Dülmen, Germany, her visions had become concerned primarily with the life of Jesus Christ, although they encompassed also the lives of many saints and other personages (some unknown as yet to history) as well as far-reaching insights into the creation, the fall, a mysterious mountain of the prophets, the spiritual hierarchies, paradise and purgatory, the heavenly Jerusalem, and much besides.

In the context of Anne Catherine's visions, and related conversations, much was said also of spiritual labors, described symbolically as work in the "nuptial house," the "inner chamber," the "garden," and the "vineyard." In this way many teachings on the inner life and prayer came forward, along with detailed accounts of healing work and journeys for "poor souls" in purgatory or in past epochs. Anne Catherine also showed considerable concern for the souls of those around her, especially her later amanuensis Clemens Brentano, in connection with his initial lack of faith.

Owing to difficult political circumstances, Anne Catherine's convent was disbanded on December 3, 1811, and one by one the nuns in residence were obliged to leave. Anne Catherine—already very ill—withdrew to a small room in a house in Dülmen. By November, 1812, her illness had grown so severe that she was permanently confined to bed. Shortly thereafter, on December 29, 1812, she received the stigmata, a manifesting of the wounds suffered by Christ on the cross, and the highest outward sign of inner union with him. Unable to assimilate any form of nourishment,

i

for the rest of her life she was sustained almost exclusively by water and the eucharist.

As news spread that she bore the stigmata (which bled on Fridays), more and more people came to see her. For us, the most significant of these was Clemens Brentano, who first visited her on Thursday morning, September 24, 1818. He was so impressed by the radiance of her being that he decided to relocate nearby in order to record her visions. Anne Catherine had already had a presentiment that someone—whom she called "the pilgrim"— would one day come to preserve her revelations. The moment Clemens Brentano entered her room, she recognized him as this pilgrim.

Brentano, a novelist and Romantic poet then living in Berlin, was associated with leading members of the Romantic Movement in Germany. He settled his affairs and moved from Berlin to Dülmen early in 1819. Thereafter he visited Anne Catherine every morning, noting down briefly all she related to him. After writing out a full report at home, he returned later the same day to read it back to her. She would then often expand upon certain points, or, if necessary, correct details.

On July 29, 1820, Anne Catherine began to communicate visions concerning the day-by-day life of Jesus. These visions encompassed the better part of his ministry, and she was able to describe in extraordinary detail the places he visited, his miracles and healings, his teaching activity in the synagogues and elsewhere, and the people around him. She not only named and described many of these people with astonishing concreteness, but spoke also of their families, their occupations, and other intimate biographical details.

It seems clear that Anne Catherine was called to relate these day-by-day details of the life and ministry of Jesus, and that Clemens Brentano was called to record all she communicated of her visions. They worked together daily until her death on February 9, 1824, except for one period of six months, during which Brentano was away, and several shorter periods when, mainly due to illness, it was impossible for Anne Catherine to communicate her visions.

⊕

ENCOUNTERING the visions of Anne Catherine Emmerich can raise the question: how is it possible that this woman, who never left the German region in which she was born and had very little education, could describe in such detail not only the story of creation; heaven, hell, and purgatory; the fall of angels and humanity; the spiritual hierarchies and saints; the Promise and the Ark of the Covenant; the apocalypse; spiritual warfare; and the heavenly Jerusalem—but *also* the geography and topography of Palestine and the customs and habits of people living there at the time of Jesus Christ? To at least partially answer this, the researcher upon whose work the *chronological* aspects of this new edition is largely based, Dr. Robert Powell, undertook an exhaustive analysis of her work, gradually laying bare the historical reality underlying the life of Jesus (see "Chronology" below). But his work was not done in isolation, for others had earlier laid some groundwork.

For example the French priest Abbé Julien Gouyet of Paris, after reading an account of Anne Catherine's visions concerning the death of the Virgin Mary near Ephesus, traveled there and searched the region. On October 18, 1881, guided by various particulars in her account, he discovered the ruins of a small stone building on a mountain (Bulbul Dag, "Mount Nightingale") overlooking the Aegean Sea with a view across to the remains of the ancient city of Ephesus. Abbé Gouyet was convinced that this was the house described in Anne Catherine's visions as the dwelling of the Virgin Mary during the last years of her life. He was at first ridiculed, but several years later the ruins were independently rediscovered by two Lazarist missionaries who had undertaken a similar search on the basis of Anne Catherine's visions. They determined that the building had been a place of pilgrimage in earlier times for Christians descended from the church of Ephesus, the community referred to by St. John (Rev. 2:1–7). The building had been known in those days as Panaya Kapulu, the house of the Blessed Virgin, and was revered as the place where she had died. Traditionally, the date of her death, August 15, was the *very day* of the annual pilgrimage to Panaya Kapulu.

That Anne Catherine's visions provide spiritual nourishment had long been the experience of many spiritual seekers, but the discovery of Panaya Kapulu confirmed that her visions could also (at least in part) be corroborated along conventional lines of research.

Sources

THE visions of Anne Catherine Emmerich have been published in English translation in various editions since late in the nineteenth century. These editions focused primarily on the visions of the life of Jesus Christ and of Mary, with some material drawn from Old Testament times also. However the *original* notes of Clemens Brentano contained material on many other fascinating subjects. Much of this material has not been readily available before now, either in German or in English translation, a gap that this twelve-volume *New Light on the Visions Anne Catherine Emmerich* series is meant at least to begin filling.

Until now the only translations available of some of this latter material appeared in the two-volume biography of Anne Catherine by Rev. Carl E. Schmöger, first published in English in 1885. Rev. Schmöger, who was also instrumental in the selection and arrangement of the visions related to the life of Jesus Christ upon which later English translations were based, included in the biography a selection of the supplemental material mentioned above —but his selection was necessarily limited.

Clemens Brentano himself was only able to compile from his notes a few volumes for publication, and upon his death the notes passed to his brother Christian, who had been an interested participant in Clemens's work with Anne Catherine from the start (in fact, Christian had arranged his brother's first meeting with the visionary). Christian, however, proved unable to coordinate the notes any further. And so the first phase of this seemingly insurmountable task fell in due course to Rev. Schmöger.

Then, in the last decades of the twentieth century, the German publisher Kohlhammer commenced publishing, under the auspices of the *Frankfurter Brentano Ausgabe*, an intended complete edition of Brentano's works, projected to number as many as sixty volumes. Part of this project was the publication of facsimiles of the thirty-eight notebooks of Brentano's notes of the visions of Anne Catherine. (Brentano also noted down details of their conversations in other contexts, as well as his own experiences while attending her.) With the Kohlhammer edition, a wider public would finally gain access to the originals upon which later compilations and translations of the visions had been based. However, this noble project has not been completed, and at present there is no indication whether it will recommence. An additional impediment for researchers in dealing with the facsimiles is the fact that Brentano's notes were penned in a now archaic German script that only specialists can read.

Thus matters stood until Jozef De Raedemaeker, a dedicated Belgian researcher, undertook the enormous task of transcribing the full body of notes from the archaic script into modern German—making it available in printed and digital form in 2009. The combined 38 notebooks exceed 7,300 pages and include many hand-drawn illustrations as well as typographic conventions to identify the contributions of others present at Anne Catherine's bedside, who sometimes took notes or added comments, and sometimes drawings.

⊕

ANYONE who does even minimal research on the visions of Anne Catherine Emmerich as depicted in the works attributed to Brentano's notes will soon discover that there are conflicting opinions regarding their fidelity to the words of Anne Catherine herself. This would be a subject in itself, but some remarks may be offered here. First, Anne Catherine, who had little formal education, spoke in a Low-German dialect that even Brentano, at the outset, had some difficulty understanding. Secondly, the material that was eventually fit together into a connected account in the published versions often represents a collation of as many as a dozen or more passages gleaned from visions separated sometimes by months, or even years. This can be partially explained by the fact that the visions were often related to events in the ecclesiastical year, to feasts of saints, to individuals with specific needs or requests, or to the presence of relics.

And so a great deal of work had to be done to organize and knit together related segments of visions, and to then arrange them in a meaningful sequence. Then again, it was deemed necessary to refine the language sufficiently to render it in a more contemporary idiom. There is, then, a legitimate concern that so famous and gifted a literary figure as Clemens Brentano might, even if unintentionally, have introduced some of his own impressions, interpretations, and sensitivities into his renditions. And a similar concern could be raised concerning Rev. Schmöger's subsequent arrangements, as well as those of later editors and translators working at yet a further remove.

Much of the debate on this subject, however, took place without ready access to the original notes, a defect that has now been remedied. At certain points in his transcriptions De Raedemaeker addresses this issue by comparing fragments of the original notes with versions of these same fragments as they appear in Rev. Schmöger's edition, after he in turn had worked, in some instances, with Brentano's own compilations from his original notes—and in some cases there are non-trivial discrepancies. This is an area that requires further research.

Perhaps I myself may be permitted to chime in here, as there are not many who have entered into this vast field, and I can at least appeal to many years of engagement with the visions of Anne Catherine, *including* examining De Raedemaeker's transcriptions of all thirty-eight notebooks. While thus occupied, I inevitably began to identify for myself many of the original sources upon which Rev. Schmöger based his versions well over a century ago, and in such cases could assess the fidelity of the latter to the former. Although such details do not lie within the scope of this series, I can say that, with very rare exceptions—especially allowing for the frequent need to splice together disparate fragments—Rev. Schmöger's renderings remain remarkably true to the original, and any minimal divergences are for the most part quite trivial, insofar as I have been able to investigate.

During this process, however, I *was* struck by the fact that considerable material had been *omitted*. This may well have been owing to the enormity of the task, as also to pagination limits set by the publisher; or also, partly a measure of Rev. Schmöger's personal judgment and concerns. Perhaps some of the excluded material seemed unintelligible to him, or even scandalous. However that may be, in this current series as much as possible of this neglected material has been extracted, translated, and incorporated in the relevant volumes.

It needs to be said also, in response to assertions (made mostly without benefit of access to his actual notes) that Brentano misrepresented Anne Catherine, or, even worse, took advantage of his notes to compile an independent literary work that might embellish his reputation, that in fact, in his notes, Brentano *candidly* reports *exactly* what he heard Anne Catherine say, *no matter how* extraordinary, puzzling, or even apparently contradictory. He himself offers many instances where only later—sometimes years after Anne Catherine had died—he (often with the help of academic experts) finally began to understand previously incomprehensible passages in the visions. He steadfastly refused—according to his own account and that of others—to edit out "difficulties," feeling himself, rather, under a sacred obligation to preserve his record intact and unaltered for posterity. And when the notes passed to his brother Christian, the latter adhered to the same policy.

Even without the benefit of access to the original notes on the part of most researchers, and even in face of an undercurrent of scepticism as to the authenticity of the visions, it may be worthwhile, in drawing this matter to a close for our present purposes, to note that on October 3, 2004, Anne Catherine was beatified by Pope John Paul II, who remarked: "Her example opened the hearts of poor and rich alike, of simple and cultured persons, whom she instructed in loving dedication to Jesus Christ." And in the Vatican's biography of Anne Catherine we read: "Her words, which have reached innumerable people in many languages from her modest room in Dülmen through the writings of Clemens Brentano are an outstanding proclamation of the gospel in service to salvation right up to the present day."

Chronology

PERHAPS the most surprising feature of this new series on Anne Catherine Emmerich will be the inclusion of *historical dates*—and so a brief discussion of this feature is offered below.

As described earlier, Anne Catherine was so attuned to the life of Jesus Christ as a mystical-historical reality that her comprehensive visions encompassed even minute details of time and place—testable "coordinates" in fact. This degree of precision was made possible by the many temporal as well as geographical descriptions and references contained in the visions—as mentioned earlier in connection with the discovery of the house of the Blessed Virgin.

Many chronologies of the life of Jesus Christ have been put forward over the centuries, but the dates offered in this current series differ from previous efforts in that they derive from the application of modern chronological and astro-chronological science to the whole of Anne Catherine's visions—which latter constitute a vast body of data internally consistent as to time and place to an extraordinary degree, so that, taking the generally agreed upon time period of Jesus's life, results of a high degree of reliability can be determined.

Naturally, the overriding value of the visions lies in the additional insight they offer into the life of Jesus Christ, so that for some the dating may represent no more than a convenient framework for study and meditation. Such readers need not trouble themselves about the specific dates, although they may nonetheless find that the chronology offers a useful way to maintain their orientation within any given volume, as also when referring to events in volumes already read. Some, however, will wish to assess for themselves the method by which specific dates have been thought reliable enough to include here. They may read elsewhere[1] the story of the determination of the chronology of the life of Jesus Christ included in these volumes.

---

[1] *The Visions of Anne Catherine Emmerich*, Book III, Appendix I (Kettering, OH: Angelico Press, 2015), which is based on the work of Dr. Robert Powell.

The New Light on the Visions
of Anne Catherine Emmerich *Series*

THE present book is one of the twelve volumes of the "New Light on the Visions of Anne Catherine Emmerich" series published by Angelico Press. This series supplements two earlier Angelico publications: *The Visions of Anne Catherine Emmerich*, Books I–III (1,700 pages in large format, with 600 illustrations and forty-three maps); and the smaller-format, slightly abridged edition: *Life, Passion, Death, & Resurrection of Jesus Christ* (*A Chronicle from the Visions of Anne Catherine Emmerich*), Books I–IV (1,770 pages with 150 illustrations and 43 maps). As described earlier, in 2009 Clemens Brentano's original notes of Anne Catherine's visions became readily available for reference. At that time the above texts were already nearing completion. With the appearance of these notes, however, the editor resolved to pause, and, to the extent possible, research this vast body of notes to ascertain what further light they might shed on what had by then been prepared for publication. While the better part of another decade was devoted to the task, much research, of course, remains to be done (see "Future Prospects" below). But at some point one must call a halt, and so, after the insertion of relevant new translations into the two sets mentioned above and their publication in 2015–2016, the present series was conceived as a means to present in various contexts such new material as has since then been selected and translated from the notes.

In general, the content of each volume of this series consists (1) of material selected by individual or theme from earlier translations—reviewed, supplemented, and revised where necessary, especially for consistency of usage; and (2) of newly selected and translated material germane to the content of that volume. With regard to both individuals and themes, the procedure was to extract every reference thus far located in the notes and in prior translations and weave them together into a connected account. The reader can thus find in one place almost all of what Anne Catherine had to say about any given individual or theme.

Virtually every individual in the biblical visions (approximately 250 in total) is referenced in the five *People of the New Testament* volumes (which include also some figures from earlier and later times). A separate volume, *The Life of the Virgin Mary*, is dedicated to Mary and her ancestry (including much on the Essenes); and another volume, *Scenes from the Lives of the Saints*, treats of fifty-nine saints. Separate volumes cover events prior to the appearance of the holy family: *First Beginnings* and *Mysteries of the Old Testament*. Two further volumes cover a multitude of separate themes: *Inner Life and Worlds of Soul & Spirit* and *Spiritual Works and Journeys*. A final volume represents a condensed, edited, rearranged, supplemented, and retypeset edition of Rev. Carl E. Schmöger's exhaustive biography of Anne Catherine, first published in English in 1885. For clarity of organization, much of this biography in its original form has been redistributed among other volumes of this series. What remains has also been enriched with newly-translated material. A list of all twelve volumes of this series appears at the conclusion of this preface.

Practical Considerations

IN view of the sometimes extensive wealth of material presented concerning certain individuals—especially major characters—a judicious essentializing of scenes has sometimes been resorted to. In some cases, especially those of closely related apostles and disciples (or others regularly treated together in the visions), rather than duplicating material, the expedient adopted was to disentangle scenes to the extent possible, so that the full story could be garnered gradually by reading the separate accounts of each. Nonetheless, since readers may jump around in their selection of individuals to study, some repetition was unavoidable in order to provide enough context to keep the separate accounts reasonably sequential and unified. Put another way, these volumes are conceived primarily as reference works to which one turns for particulars on specific persons or themes rather than as connected narratives to be read cover to cover. Of course, the volumes may be read in the latter fashion also, in which case the occasional repeated material will be more noticeable.

Another consideration was that some individuals play so great a role in the visions (e.g., John the Baptist, St. Joseph, Peter, Matthew, Judas, and the Virgin Mary) that it would be impractical to include every mention in a chronological itinerary. Emphasis in such cases has been placed primarily on more general and newly-translated material. Inquisitive readers can of course turn to the index of the large-format, three-volume *The Visions of Anne Catherine Emmerich* to expand their research on such individuals.

It must be well understood that all the editor could do was work with what Anne Catherine actually said. Some little-known (or even totally unknown) individuals may enjoy longer accounts in these volumes than other, very well known, figures from the gospels or later Christian tradition! There can be no question of assigning relative importance to any individual based solely upon how extensive Anne Catherine's visions of that person may have been. Likewise, stories may have gaps, or sometimes end abruptly. It is indeed unfortunate that (as Brentano repeatedly laments in his notes) so much was lost owing to Anne Catherine's considerable suffering, household distractions, and the many obligations laid upon her—all of which interfered with her visions and her capacity to recall them. And yet withal, how much we have to be grateful for!

To streamline as far as possible a complex text, these usages were established: The voice of the narrator (Rev. Schmöger) is put in italics. Direct citations from Brentano (and a few others) are put in quotes. Anne Catherine's text bears no quotation indicators *except* where references to her words are embedded in the two contexts just mentioned. Parentheses enclose supplemental material from Anne Catherine or Brentano; brackets enclose material from Rev. Schmöger or the present editor. Footnotes from the hand of Brentano are followed by CB; those consisting of further visionary content from Anne Catherine are—for clarity in this context—enclosed in quotation marks; all other unattributed footnotes have been supplied by the present editor, sometimes incorporating what seemed worth retaining from notes by others in earlier editions.[1]

---

[1] The most useful material of this sort has been integrated from notes to a version of *The Life of the Virgin Mary* provided by Rev. Sebastian Bullough, O.P., to whom we express our gratitude.

For convenience, especially in itineraries of individuals, dates are incorporated in what is otherwise purely Anne Catherine's visionary text. It must, however, be well understood that these dates are derivative, as mentioned in "Chronology" above, *not* from the hand of Anne Catherine. As another help, for many major figures, summaries are provided at the outset. These are often in the third person—as they represent a condensation by the editor—but are nonetheless derived directly from the visions.

In such a context as these visions represent, capitalization (a topic upon which there are many and various usages, and often passionate opinions) represented a particular challenge. In the end, after experimenting with progressively increasing degrees of simplification, it was determined—in order not to overly fatigue the reader of what essentially amounts to an extended narrative rather than devotional reading properly speaking—to implement a very spare policy indeed, reserving capitalization to the Deity, and to certain terms that in Anne Catherine's visions assume a unique significance, such as the Ark of the Covenant, and what she calls the Promise, or sometimes the Holy Thing, the Mystery or Sacrament (in this special sense), or even the Germ or Seed. Finally, in cases where more general considerations are followed by chronological extracts forming a connected itinerary, the break is signaled by a row of five typographic crosses.

Prospects for the Future

AS editor of this series I am only too aware of my limitations in the face of the awe-inspiring magnitude of the task. My initial inspiration was solely the *spiritual value* of Anne Catherine's visions as a means to help seekers find their way *back* to a faithful connection with Jesus Christ; or, in the case of so many in our time, find their way *for the first time* to a dawning awareness of what they may thus far have failed to see. Further, there are great, resonant depths in the visions, like choirs of symbolism. As time went on I could only go deeper, entering upon the work that has led now, finally, to completing this series. Along with spiritual benefits and guidance, it was and will ever remain also a thrilling journey of discovery. Now, with Brentano's original notes available thanks to the efforts of Jozef De Raedemaeker, there are further depths to explore, as alas—despite so many years of work—the rich sod has only been broken.

In the visions will be found fascinating indications and hints for archeologists, historians, linguists, theologians, students of comparative religion, chronologists, specialists in symbolism, and more. Over and above the *primary element* of spiritual inspiration, it is my hope that such specialists may in due course take up these visions (including the entire corpus of Brentano's notes) and press further forward. How one would love to see a foundation, a university, a religious sodality, or some private individual or group sponsor so important and propitious a project. If the largely solitary results presented here serve to advance such future research, if hearts and souls are moved and enriched by *The Anne Catherine Emmerich Series* as a whole, the effort will have achieved its primary purpose.

JAMES RICHARD WETMORE

Acknowledgments

IT is difficult to sift out elements from earlier translators of these visions, but our main debt of gratitude for much of the English text taken as a foundation in the current work is owed to Sir Michael Palairet. Incalculable thanks are owed to Jozef De Raedemaeker for his past and present work with the original handwritten notes of Clemens Brentano. Occasional assistance with translation was received from Mado Spiegler, James Morgante, and especially Harrie Salman. A special thanks goes to Robert Powell, who has been a companion at every stage of this journey owing to his dedication to Anne Catherine in every respect: researching, translating when necessary, and, preeminently, applying his skills to the task of establishing the chronology that has been incorporated in this edition (in which connection Fr. Helmut Fahsel should also be mentioned). Most line drawings in the volumes are taken from Brentano's notes; the occasional paintings included are from the hand of James J. Tissot, as are all but one of the cover illustrations.

The New Light on the Visions
of Anne Catherine Emmerich Series

From Joseph & Asenath
to the
Prophet Malachi

Joseph and His Brethern Welcomed by Pharaoh

From Joseph and Asenath
to the Prophet Malachi

Joseph and Asenath

JOSEPH was fifteen years old when he was sold into Egypt. He was of middle height, very slender and agile, active both in body and mind. He was indeed very different from his brothers, and all felt drawn to love him. Were it not for the marked preference shown him by his father, his brothers also would have loved him. Joseph wore his hair divided into three, one part on either side of his head, the third falling down behind in long curls. When ruler over Egypt, he wore it short, but afterward allowed it again to grow.

As has been said, when Jacob bestowed the many-colored coat upon Joseph, he gave over to him also some of the bones of Adam, without telling him, however, what they were.[1] Jacob gave them to Joseph as a precious talisman, for he knew well that his brothers did not love him. Joseph carried the bones on his breast in a little leathern bag rounded on top. When his brothers sold him, they took from him only the colored coat and his customary outer garment but left the band and a sort of scapular on his breast, beneath which he had hung the little bag. The colored coat was white with broad red stripes. It had on the breast three rows of black cord crossing one another, in the center of which were yellow ornaments. It was full around the breast. When bound at the waist, the fullness served as a pocket. It was narrower toward the lower part of the skirt and had slits at the side to render motion easier. It fell below the knee and was somewhat

---

[1] However, when later Jacob went to Egypt and Joseph asked him about the talisman his father had earlier entrusted him with, he revealed to him that the bones were those of Adam.

longer in the back and open in front. Joseph's ordinary dress did not reach to the knees.

Joseph was known to Pharaoh and his wife before his imprisonment.[1] Potiphar's affairs were so flourishing under Joseph's management—and Potiphar himself was so blessed during Joseph's stay under his roof, since he conducted all things so well for Pharaoh—that the latter was eager to see the faithful servant.[2] Pharaoh's wife, who was religiously inclined and very desirous of salvation, and who had at the same time—like all Egyptians—a great hankering after new gods, was so astounded at the wise, intelligent, extraordinary young stranger that she honored him interiorly as a divinity. She said repeatedly to Pharaoh: "This man has been sent by our gods. He is not a human being like ourselves."

Hence it came to pass that Joseph was thrown, not into the common dungeon, but into the prison reserved for the nobility, and there made overseer in the final years of his incarceration, which lasted seven years in total. During his greatest affliction he received the mysterious Blessing of Jacob in the same manner as the patriarchs had done. He had a vision also of a numerous posterity.

Pharaoh's wife sincerely deplored his conviction as a malefactor and at first thought she had been mistaken in him. But when he was liberated and again appeared at court she treated him with great distinction.[3]

---

[1] Anne Catherine remarked that it seemed odd to her that holy scripture does not mention that Joseph had long been acquainted with Pharaoh and his wife before he was imprisoned.

[2] Potiphar is said the have been the captain of the palace guard of the Pharaoh. He is cited in Genesis 39:1 as the one who purchased Joseph as a household slave from his brothers.

[3] The cup that Joseph ordered to be placed in Benjamin's sack was the first present the queen had made to him. I know it well; it had two handles, but no foot. It seemed to have been cut out of one precious stone, or one solid transparent mass—I know not which—and was in shape exactly like the upper part of the chalice used at the Last Supper. It was among the vessels the children of Israel took away with them from Egypt, and was afterward preserved in the Ark of the Covenant.

I know all about Potiphar's wife. I saw how desirous she was to seduce Joseph; but after his elevation, she did penance and became chaste and devout. She was a tall, powerful woman, her skin of a yellowish-brown and shining like silk. She wore a colored robe over which was one of figured gauze. The lower one shone through it as if through lace. Joseph had frequent contact with her, since his master's affairs were all entrusted to him. But when he became aware of the fact that she had grown more familiar in her manner toward him, he no longer remained in the house overnight during his master's absence. She often intruded herself upon him when he was busy at his writing. Once I saw her enter his presence in immodest attire. He was standing writing in one corner of a hall.[1] She addressed him and he replied. Then she grew bolder, seeing which he turned hurriedly away. She grasped his mantle but he fled leaving it in her hand. This scene did not transpire in her chamber, nor was there anywhere in evidence a bed.

I saw Joseph with Potiphar's pagan priests at Heliopolis. Asenath, the daughter of Dinah[2] and the Shechemite, lived with them as a prophetess and a decorator of the idols. Seven other maidens were her companions. Potiphar had bought her from her nurse in her fifth year.[3] This nurse had fled with her to the Red Sea by order of Jacob, that the child might not be murdered by his sons. Asenath possessed the spirit of prophecy and was esteemed by Potiphar as a prophetess. Joseph knew her, but he knew not that she was his niece.[4] She was of a very earnest character, sought seclusion, and in spite of her great beauty abhorred the society of men.

Asenath was favored with significant visions, was familiar with the Egyptian star worship, and had a secret presentiment of the

[1] A related note states that in those days scribes used to write upon rolls of parchment that hung on the wall. The scribe either sat or stood before them.

[2] The daughter of Jacob.

[3] "At the time she was sold by Jacob, I saw Asenath as a beautiful child, naked but for a cloth wrapped about her."

[4] Elsewhere Anne Catherine says: "Joseph knew of Asenath's wisdom. He was twenty-five years of age when they married. Their family connection was still a mystery to them. Asenath did not see it."

religion of the patriarchs. I saw no witchcraft connected with her. She saw in vision the whole mystery of life, the transplanting, the coming to, and the departure of Israel from Egypt—even the long journey through the wilderness. With a stylus she wrote many rolls on the leaves of a water-plant or on skin. The letters were strange-looking, they were like the heads of birds and animals. She was familiar with the stars and could foretell individual destinies.

Asenath's writings were, even during her lifetime, misunderstood by the Egyptians and misconstrued into a sanction for their wicked practices. Indeed, they led to much scandal, especially her visions regarding the divine Seed and its history in humankind. It was all expressed in images—as visions are—and was misunderstood. Later, she and Joseph consigned to the flames many of these writings still in her possession. Asenath grieved deeply over these misconceptions brought about by the evil one, and she shed many tears.[1] Alongside her writings, she was experienced also in the application of healing herbs and other simples.

Moses possessed many of the writings of Asenath, which he made use of in his own works,[2] and it was through her that he learned much regarding the journey through the desert and many events that occurred along the way.

Asenath had more numerous visions than any other of her time and was filled with wondrous wisdom. She conducted herself gravely, and refused advice to none. She could weave also, and embroider. By reading the stars she could anticipate the flooding of the Nile. Her enlightened spirit detected humankind's corruption of truth—for which reason she was grave, reserved, retiring, and silent.

I saw that the misconception of Asenath's visions and writings led to her being worshipped under the name of Isis, and Joseph under that of Osiris. This perhaps was the cause of her abundant

---

[1] "I have seen the pagan priests introduced into strange, diabolical worlds, where they beheld the most abominable things. By such diabolical visions were the secret communications of Asenath disfigured and made to contribute to the abominations of idolatry."

[2] Anne Catherine's words here were not entirely clear upon this point.

tears. She wrote also against the Egyptians' erroneous conception of her visions, which had led to their proclaiming her the mother of all the gods.

When Potiphar offered sacrifice, Asenath ascended a tower upon which was a garden. Here she gazed upon the stars by moonlight. She fell into ecstasy and read all things clearly in the stars. The truth was shown her in pictures, because she was chosen of God.

Asenath introduced many useful arts and domestic animals into Egypt; among the latter, for instance, the cow. She taught the arts of making cheese, of weaving, and many others hitherto unknown to the inhabitants. She also healed many diseases. The plow was introduced by Joseph, who was himself skilled in its use.[1]

There was one thing that seemed truly wonderful to me. Asenath ordered the flesh of the numerous animals slaughtered for sacrifice to be boiled down until it became a gelatinous mass, which served for food on campaigns and in times of scarcity. The operation was carried on in the open air and in caldrons in the earth.[2] The Egyptians were rejoiced and amazed at this new mode of procuring food. She provided them also a means to multiply grains.[3]

When Joseph met Asenath at the pagan priest's dwelling, she approached to embrace or kiss him. This she did not through boldness, but impelled by the spirit. It was in her a kind of prophetic action, and took place in presence of the pagan priest. Asenath was looked upon as holy, but I saw Joseph keep her off with outstretched hand and address earnest words to her. Then

---

[1] "Joseph introduced the plow in various places throughout Egypt. He himself plowed, and did everything with ease. It was not permitted to yoke ox and cow together. Often a sacrifice would quite suddenly be offered before the plow."

[2] Brentano adds this note: "This could be the tablets of bouillon next to the Tablet of Isis." But the reference is unclear to this editor.

[3] Brentano here adds: "Did she mean by this expression to increase or multiply the Israelites, or the seeds? For she said this following her observation that Asenath, after bearing eighteen children, had mourned Joseph's [subsequent] infertility."

Asenath, deeply agitated, retired to her own room, where she remained in tears and penance.

I saw her in her chamber. She stood concealed by a curtain, her wealth of long, beautiful hair cascading around her and curling at the ends. Basins with warm and cold water stood by, and she was washing herself. There was impressed on the skin of the pit of her stomach a wonderful sign. In a figure like a heart-shaped shell stood a child with outstretched arms, holding in one hand a small dish, in the other a cup, or chalice. In the dish were three young ears of corn that appeared to be just breaking out of the husk, and the figure of a little bird that seemed to peck after the grapes in the cup held by the child.[1]

As Asenath stood there washing herself I saw an angel appear in resplendent raiment, holding in his hand a blossom that signified mystery.[2] It was a lotus. He saluted Asenath. She glanced at him and drew her veil around her. I no longer recall the exact words, but he commanded her to dry her tears and adorn herself in festal robes; he also requested her to bring him food.

---

[1] "Jacob knew of this sign; but notwithstanding, he had to send the child away in order to shield her from the rage of his sons. But when he came down into Egypt, and Joseph told him all things, he recognized his granddaughter by this mark. Joseph too had a mark of the same kind upon his breast, a very full bunch of grapes." On another occasion Anne Catherine added the following: "Joseph also had a singular mark upon his stomach region: a growth like a cluster with many little tubercles was attached there by a cord or peduncle, signifying his many descendents. In the countryside where I lived we sometimes call such growths 'veen,' about which we have a saying that children who bear such a mark will be either significant or happy. When they appear among us we tie off the growths so as to remove them. My own father had such a growth on his fibula, though in his case there was nothing fortunate about it."

Brentano adds here the following note: "Eutychius of Alexandria writes that Joseph had a mark upon his shoulder as a sign of prophecy (Baumgarten, *Allgemeine Welthistorie*, II, p. 350). In a strange way this fits in with the fact that Asenath often called the ears of corn that she brought with her into the world (on the skin of her stomach) ears of prophecy, or wisdom, explaining that she would have had much clearer visions had these growths not been tied off. Also, Anne Catherine said that the prophets of old usually bore such special marks."

[2] "The flowers were yellow and of an unusual kind, divided into two sexes below the water, but upon rising to the surface they would come together and as it were unite as one."

Asenath left the room and returned adorned as directed, bringing with her a low table, small and light, upon which were wine and little flat loaves that had been baked in ashes. Asenath evinced no fear. She was not shy, but simple and humble—just like Abraham and the other patriarchs—when treating with apparitions. When the angel now spoke to her, she unveiled.

He desired of her some honey, but she replied that, unlike other maidens who are fond of it, she had none. Thereupon the angel told her that she would find some among the idols that stood in her chamber. These small, swaddled idols were of various forms; they had heads of animals and for bodies serpents coiled downward. Asenath herself made such figures.

Asenath looked, and found a beautiful, coarse-celled honeycomb, white as the host of our altars. She set it before the angel, who bade her eat of it. He blessed it, and I saw it shining and flashing between them.

I cannot now express the signification of this heavenly honey; for when one sees such things, it is just as they actually are, one knows all. But now, when I try to recall it, the honey appears to be what is called honey, yet I know not what the flowers, the bees, and the honey properly signified. I can only say this much: Asenath really possessed in herself only bread and wine,[1] but no honey. By the reception of this honey, she issued from idolatry into the light of Israel. It signified also that she should aid many souls, that many, like bees, should build around her. I heard her say that she would drink no more wine, for that now she was more in need of honey. I saw numbers of bees and vast stores of honey in Midian, near Jethro.

In blessing the honeycomb that Asenath found among the small idols, the angel directed his finger toward all regions of the world, which signified how by her presence, by her being a model for others, and by the mystery of the honeycomb, she should be a mother and a leader. When later on she was honored as a divinity and represented with numerous breasts, it was in

---

[1] Or that which is typified by bread and wine.

consequence of the misconception of her vision that she should nourish many.

The angel told her that she was destined to be the bride of Joseph and should be united with him in the same way as lotus flowers float together and become one. And he blessed her along the following lines: he motioned with his hand from her head down over the middle of her body, then over the right breast to the left breast to the heart, and then from the right hip to the left hip to her lap (see drawing).[1]

This was apparently a blessing of her receiving, birthing, and nourishing, because he blessed her lap and her breast.[2]

After this I saw in vision Joseph going to Potiphar to demand Asenath for his wife; but I can only remember that, like the angel, he carried a lotus in his hand. Joseph knew of Asenath's wonderful wisdom but their mutual family relationship was hidden from both.

I saw that Pharaoh's son likewise was in love with Asenath, on which account she had to remain secluded. He had persuaded Dan and Gad[3] to espouse his cause, and all three lay in ambush to slay Joseph. But Judah (obeying a divine inspiration, I think) warned Joseph to take another route. Benjamin also conducted himself nobly in this affair, and defended Asenath. Dan and Gad were punished by the death of their children. Joseph and Asenath had been forewarned by God before any others knew of the scheme. This took place just at the time when the two were becoming ever more highly honored in Egypt.

At this very juncture I saw Joseph and Asenath riding by in a chariot, all-shining in face of that danger. Asenath wore a completely golden breastpiece from below the arms. It must have

---

[1] "As Isaac had blessed Jacob, and as the angel had blessed Abraham. The three lines that constituted the formula of that blessing were drawn upon her twice, once to the pit of the stomach and once to the abdomen."

[2] It is perhaps the more remarkable that Anne Catherine herself, as also a stigmatized Italian woman, had upon their breasts such a double cross, which often became visible and bled.

[3] Two sons of Jacob, brothers to Joseph.

been uncomfortable to wear, for it was tight-fitting, holding up from below—as in an arch—the breasts, which from above were covered chastely with many necklaces of pearls and other ornaments. Upon the breastpiece were many figures and signs. Her dress reached to her knees, below which the limbs were tightly laced. A wide mantle fell over the back, the sides of which were clasped together over the knees. The toes of her shoes were turned up like skates, and her headdress of colored feathers and pearls was shaped like a helmet.[1]

On his upper body Joseph wore a tight-fitting coat with sleeves, and over it a golden breastplate covered with figures. Straps with golden knots were crossed around the hips, and from his shoulders fell a mantle. His head ornament was of feathers and precious stones.

When Joseph and Asenath appeared in public, they—like the pagan priests of Potiphar—bore in their hand a symbol regarded as sacred and emblematic of the highest authority.[2] The upper part was a ring; the lower, a Latin cross, a T, like this:

It served as a seal, and when grain was measured and divided, the heaps were marked with it. It was used in the same way for the building of granaries and canals, also for the rising and falling of the Nile. Writings were sealed with it after they had first been marked with a red vegetable juice. When Joseph discharged any

---

[1] The description here, particularly of Asenath is, in Brentano's notes, more generally applied to women, as follows: "Egyptian women wore caps of feathers, or worked colorful feathers and pearls into their hair. Often their bare breasts were covered with coral and fringe. Over pants they wore short, pleated skirts; and over all, wide, flowing mantles with many folds. On their bare arms were rings, as also (with the addition of chains) around their torso and legs; their footwear consisted of low and high heels, and beaked shoes."

[2] Other people wore different signs.

official duty, this symbol of authority—the cross being clasped in the ring—lay on a cushion at his side, like this:

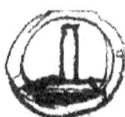

It seemed to me also like a distinctive sign of the mystery of the Ark of the Covenant still enclosed in Joseph.[1] Asenath also had an instrument like a wand:

When in vision, she followed wherever it led. Where it quivered, she struck the earth, and so discovered springs and water. It was made under the influence of the stars.

There were exemplars of this symbol in larger and smaller sizes. They were used in the construction of canals, and were associated with the rising of the waters of the Nile. The doors to the granaries bore this sign also. Asenath's wand was one such as is used to dowse for water, dig wells, and locate other sites. This instrument was fabricated in accordance with stellar influences.

Anne Catherine added at this point: It is a symbol, but one that is also like a cross, and I was told something about this.

The pilgrim then brought to her a cruciform image bearing a remarkable resemblance to this symbol, reproduced in T. Cornelli Curtii Augustiniani de Claris Dominicis Liber, Antverpiae 1670, p. 38, in which appears not only the

but, as an ornament on the breast, the symbol inverted as and *also the alpha and omega on the head.*

---

[1] "The pagans knew more deep mysteries, which is why there were more atrocities among them. God enshrouded the mystery of the Ark of the Covenant with fire, in order to protect it."

Text Underneath: *The Cross of Nicodemus, carved from cedar wood, venerated in Lucca.*

When Joseph went to Egypt, New Memphis was being built about seven leagues north of Old Memphis. Between the two cities, built on a dyke, was a highway with walking paths. Scattered among the trees were idols with grave, sad female faces and the bodies of dogs. They sat upon stone slabs. There were as yet no beautiful buildings, only great, long ramparts and artificial stone mountains [pyramids] full of vaults and chambers. The dwellings were slight, with a superstructure of wood. There were still great forests and marshes all around.[1]

The Egyptians worshipped all kinds of animals, toads, serpents, crocodiles. They looked on quite coolly while a person was being devoured by a crocodile, honoring it all the while. They

---

[1] "At the time of the flight of Mary into Egypt, the Nile had already changed its course."

11

worshipped the onion also, on account if its strong fragrance as well as their belief that it strengthened the powers of reproduction. At Joseph's coming, the worship of the bull had not yet come into practice. It was introduced in consequence of Pharaoh's dream of the seven fat and the seven lean kine. They had numerous kinds of idols; some like swaddled children, others like coiled serpents, some of which could be made longer or shorter at pleasure. A great many of the idols were adorned with breastplates on which the plans of cities and the course of the Nile were curiously inscribed. These shields were made in accordance with the pictures the pagan priests traced in the stars, and after whose plan they built cities and canals. New Memphis was founded in this way.

Hereafter the two towns of Memphis, and a more remote town on the Nile [she means Thebes] were built. In the one Memphis lived the Pharaoh, the other Memphis lying more to the north.

Later she describes this in a different way: New Memphis lies about seven hours from Old Memphis, meaning that it is now Cairo (at this point she drew the following map upon her bedcover).

Anne Catherine believed that New Memphis, as well as the city of Babylon,[1] was built during Joseph's lifetime and was of much service to the Jews:

Their lands [Goshen] between [the cities of] On and Bubastis had shifted more toward the latter. Joseph's grave was situated between On and Babylon on the one side [of the Nile], and Memphis on the other. Between Old Memphis and New Memphis were the most beautiful roads and side alleys built upon dykes. Situated among these latter, set upon a long stone slab, rested a massive figure with the form of a woman to the front, and of a dog behind. It was beautiful, but solemn, and seemed sad.

The evil spirits at that time must have possessed a different, a more material power, for I saw that Egyptian sorcery came out of the earth, out of the abyss. When a pagan priest began his enchantments I saw figures of all kinds of ugly animals arise out of the ground around the sorcerer and enter his mouth in a current of black vapor. He became thereby entranced and clairvoyant. It was as if, at the entrance of each spirit, a world hitherto closed was opened up to him and he saw things far and near—the abysses of the earth, countries, human beings, in fine, all things over which each particular spirit exerted an influence.[2] What the wizard saw by the aid of these spirits appeared like a delusion, a mirage, which they conjured up before him. I could see far beyond these pictures, for they were like shadows. It was as if one looked behind a curtain.

When the Egyptian pagan priests intended to read the stars, they fasted as a preparation, performed certain purifications, clothed themselves in sackcloth, and sprinkled themselves with ashes—for if impure, they could achieve nothing. While they gazed upon the stars from their tower, sacrifices were offered in the second or third storey, where there was an arrangement rather like a garden. They would observe the stars while the moon was shining. They would be transported; indeed, even should the por-

---

[1] That is, the Egyptian city of that name (near present-day Cairo), not the great Mesopotamian city with the tower.

[2] "Modern witchcraft always appears to me to be more under the influence of the spirits of the air."

tion of stars upon which they gazed be no larger than a dinner plate, they could clearly discern all therein, which they would afterward draw upon paper shields. Through such visions as these, often times sites for cities and canals were determined.

The pagans of those times had a confused knowledge of the religious mysteries of the True God that had been handed down from Seth, Enoch, Noah, and the patriarchs to the chosen people—therefore were there so many abominations in their idolatry. The devil made use of them (as later on of heresy) to weave the pure, unclouded, authentic revelations of God into a snare for humankind's destruction. Therefore God enveloped the mystery of the Ark of the Covenant in fire in order to preserve it.

As has been mentioned before,[1] when Jacob went into Egypt to Joseph, he pursued the same route through the wilderness by which later Moses journeyed to the promised land. Jacob knew that he would see Joseph again; he always had a presentiment of this in his heart. He had even had on his journey to Mesopotamia—at the place upon which he erected the altar (not where he saw the ladder)—a vision of his future sons. One he saw, in the region where Joseph was sold, sink from sight and like a star rise again in the south. He exclaimed therefore when they brought him the blood-stained coat—the foregoing circumstance almost forgotten recurring to him—"I shall weep for Joseph until I find him again."[2]

Jacob dwelt about a day's journey distant from Joseph. When he fell ill, Joseph drove in a chariot to see him. Jacob questioned him closely about Asenath, and when he heard of the sign on her person exclaimed, "She is flesh of thy flesh. She is bone of thy bone!" Then he revealed to Joseph who she was. Joseph was so deeply affected that he almost lost consciousness. On his return

---

[1] Here we duplicate some material from "Jacob" in *First Beginnings* for convenient reference.

[2] "Through Rueben, Jacob had made many inquiries as to whom Joseph had married, but had not yet been entirely enlightened on the point that Joseph's wife was his own niece. Rueben and Potiphar were old acquaintances. Owing to the influence of the former, the latter received circumcision and served the God of Jacob."

home he told his wife, and both shed tears to their heart's content over the news.

Again, as told also in the full account of Jacob, some time after, Jacob grew worse, and Joseph was again by his side. Jacob shifted his feet from the couch to the floor, and Joseph was required to lay his hand under his father's hip and swear to bury him in Canaan. While Joseph swore this oath Jacob adored the Blessing concealed within him—for he well knew that Joseph had received from an angel the Blessing that had been withdrawn from himself. Joseph bore this Blessing in his right side until death. Even after death it lay enclosed in his body until the night before the departure of the Israelites, when Moses took possession of it and placed it in the Ark of the Covenant—together with the remains of Joseph—as the Sacred Thing of the chosen people. Three months after this visit, Jacob died. Both Jews and Egyptians celebrated his obsequies and sounded his praises, for he was greatly loved.

Upon his own death, Joseph was embalmed by the Jews in the presence of the Egyptians. These connections with the Mystery must be related to a revelation that had been vouchsafed Asenath. (This seemed not to be entirely a secret, or at least a secret held by the priests, because the whole atrocious cult around the lingam [male member] as well as the cult of Isis and Osiris point to that. This probably also accounts for the intense persecution of the Israelites by Pharaoh that followed.)[1]

Later, Anne Catherine amplified upon the scene just described as follows: Joseph, at his death, was embalmed by the Jews in the presence of the Egyptians. Then were placed together the remains of Joseph and Asenath in compliance with the notes the latter had made from her visions and left to the Jews.[2]

---

[1] "Among the symbols of the Egyptians is the triangle, which for them signifies many things, especially the deepest mysteries; but as to these, I have forgotten the better part of what I was shown." The triangle is easily misunderstood, a conclusion Anne Catherine reached from a pre-biblical (pre-Esdra) codex on the Egyptian mysteries, which she once saw in vision in Armenia, adding that it was still extant.

[2] On another occasion Anne Catherine said: "Joseph, at his death, was embalmed in the presence of the Egyptians, during which process miraculous revelations of Asenath were observed. At this time a portion of the viscera from

The Egyptian priests and astrologers had placed Joseph and Asenath among their own divinities. They had some inkling of the notes left by Asenath and a presentiment of the high influence, the blessing that she and Joseph would be for Israel. But that blessing they coveted for themselves, and therefore they sought to oppress Israel. It was on this account that the Israelites, who multiplied astonishingly after Joseph's death, were so harassed by Pharaoh. The Egyptians knew well that the Israelites would not leave the country without the bones of Joseph; consequently at several different times they stole some of the remains of Joseph and at last got entire possession of them. The Jewish people at large knew only of Joseph's corpse but not of the Mystery that it contained. That was known to only a few. But the entire nation grieved deeply when the ancients found out and made known to them that the Holy Thing upon which the Promise rested had been stolen.

Joseph and Asenath were considered most holy by both the Egyptians and the Jews, and because they represented to the Egyptians in particular the fulfillment of many contorted, mysterious, and misunderstood Egyptian prophecies and archetypes, for them any remains of their bodies were considered the holiest of relics. On account of their wisdom, prophecies, and miracles, Joseph and Asenath became gods for the Egyptians. Furthermore, through their union, a turning-point in the great religious mystery of all the peoples of the Old Testament was fulfilled— namely, the task of preparing the hereditary lineage according to the flesh for the messiah upon earth.

When Jacob had wrestled with the angel, the Blessing was taken from him. It was the Blessing that had been bestowed by God first upon the patriarchs and then passed on through the firstborn of each succeeding generation—the holy Germ of the seed of the woman[1] who should tread on the head of the serpent. It was taken from Jacob and passed on to Joseph in a vision while

---

the [previously embalmed] body of Asenath was placed within the mummy of Joseph. This portion was first slit open along one side, and into it parts of Joseph's body were laid."

[1] That is, the Virgin Mary.

he was imprisoned. Following this, Israel, now no longer being a family but a nation, the Mystery also was no longer transmitted from father to [firstborn] son. Instead, when the nation received, with Moses, a religion—an Ark of the Covenant—the Holy Thing stood under the protection of divine fire. The nuptial mystery of the patriarchs became the church mystery of the Israelites, for the nation had already to a large degree become one single body.

Regarding Jacob's worshipping in this verse,[1] *where so many interpretations have been proposed, and which in the Septuagint*[2] *reads "He worshipped the top of Joseph's scepter," Anne Catherine spoke with some uncertainty, and did not discount that it was the Holy Thing in Joseph that he worshipped, which Jacob had received and which the angel with whom he had wrestled earlier in his life had taken from him.*

From Joseph's death to the departure of Israel from Egypt there were about one hundred and seventy years according to our manner of reckoning. But they had at that time another way of reckoning, other weeks and years. This was often explained to me, but I cannot now recall it. While the Israelites lived in Egypt they had no temple but only tents. They piled up stones, poured oil over them, sacrificed grain and lambs, sang, and prayed.[3]

Asenath died three years before Joseph[4] and was embalmed by Jewish women. As long as Joseph lived, her body stood in his own dedicated burial monument. But the ancients of the people, those who presided over the mysteries of their race, had taken some part of her inner organs,[5] which they preserved in a little golden

---

[1] Genesis 47:31, referred to also in Hebrews 11:21.

[2] The Greek translation of the Old Testament, which differs significantly from modern translations.

[3] More of the story of Joseph and Asenath regarding their remains and the Ark of the Covenant will by found in this volume in "Moses," "Segola," and in "The Ark of the Covenant" in *First Beginnings*.

[4] "Asenath had borne to Joseph first Manasseh and Ephraim, then other children, in all eighteen, among them several twins."

[5] On one occasion Anne Catherine mentioned the spleen and liver, another time specifying also the reproductive organs (Brentano has "vagina"), which was, she added, the "outer skin of the Mystery."

figure; and as the Egyptians also aspired to its possession, it was entrusted to the Jewish midwives. One of these women placed it in a reed box smeared with pitch and concealed it in the bulrushes near a canal where the Jews used many a nook and cranny as a hiding place. On the night of the departure [of Moses and the children of Israel from Egypt] a midwife of the tribe of Asher brought this Secret Thing to Moses. The woman's name was Sarah.

The union of their mutual Blessing rested also upon visions. Asenath's corpse remained, I believe, in Egypt. The Egyptians lay claim to it (as also to that of Joseph) and they stole her body several times. In the end they had full possession of it. The midwives were able to retain only the outer reproductive organ of Asenath, which they hid, and which finally came to light again through the agency of Sarah of the tribe of Asher, as has been said, on the night of the departure [from Egypt].[1] The people only knew of the bodily remains of Joseph, but not of the Mystery it harbored.

The Israelites and Egyptians divided the remains of Joseph among themselves, but this led to conflict, and the Mystery was clandestinely stolen from the Israelites by Egyptians. The Israelites [still] possessed the spleen and liver, and drank water in which these organs had been immersed. The store of Seed comprised within Joseph and Asenath was boundless. The Mystery laid within the Ark of the Covenant was enclosed in a transparent covering and wrapped in delicate fabrics. The Blessing it contained would wax and wane with the passage of time, according to the devotion of humankind and the grace of God. It seemed

---

[1] "Now, there was a religious mystery of the race: the women drank water [in which the bodily remains had been immersed]; they took in something, and through this had heightened fertility and easier childbirth. Again, as was said, this Mystery was preserved in the figure of a little golden mummy, rather like a swaddled babe. The Holy Anne did not drink water in which the Holy Thing had been immersed. The Blessing was *already in her*. Her first daughter [Mary Heli] was not the child of promise. Afterward, Anne fell into a long period of infertility. Then Joachim finally received a New Blessing in the Holiness [in the Temple]—not from the Ark of the Covenant, but from an angel." Elsewhere, Anne Catherine says: "He [the angel] reached into the Ark, and gave it to him [Joachim]."

always to increase in connection with sacrifice, with the blood shed by animals sacrificed upon the altar.

The Mystery of the Blessing in Connection with Joseph and Asenath

THE Mystery of the children of Israel in the time of the patriarchs rested upon the procreation of a sacred nation, that of the promised Redeemer according to the flesh. From God, Abraham received a sacred procreation that was sealed by circumcision. God promised Abraham that through his seed all the peoples of the earth would be blessed. In this way, then, did procreation and its organs—in Abraham—establish the foundation for the Blessing of God and of the coming Redeemer. What all people felt (even if they could not express it) as grounds for shame—that is, a reminder, full of mystery, of their abasement through the fall into sin—was to become instead, through the consummation of marriage by the patriarchs, through the Promise of Blessing, and through circumcision, the object of holiest awe. And because as yet there was no Sacred Thing, no Ark of the Covenant, the patriarch Abraham—by virtue of the Promise resting upon him—had his sworn [servant] Eliezer lay his hand upon his hip and swear an oath. And later the ailing Jacob turned around in his bed and worshipped the Sacred Thing in Joseph (represented by the top of his scepter).

Now, as has been said before, in the marriage of Joseph and Asenath, the promise of a family became the promise of the nations; and after their deaths, Israel broke loose like a swarm of bees out of Egypt, flying into the desert, taking with them the Mystery of Joseph, and that of Asenath as their queen. The people knew naught of all this. God's Promise, which rested upon the Mystery, surrounded the people with fear and might. With Joseph and Asenath, the mystery of procreation was raised to a higher level of dignity and entered into the Ark of the Covenant as a unity of the divided sexes, for this mystery was the [very] dwelling place [that is, Presence] among humankind of God, Who is not of one sex but is the Creator Himself. Not only this, but the object of all the divine preparations in [the time of] the

19

Old Testament was the [eventual] appearance of the Holy Virgin, who could conceive in the flesh—by the working of the Holy Spirit—the Son of God.

The entire mystery, the whole task of all religions, all re-bindings to God, was the Promise of a Redeemer and the preparation of his mother after the flesh. The whole of humanity had this Promise as a concept that was more or less clear as regards its full *truth*—but Abraham and the people of Israel that issued from him had it in *reality*. For this reason we see among them the mystery fully concealed and clothed and armed against all temptation to lascivious servitude. And we see among other peoples something shameless and atrocious emerging in all their concupiscence, regardless how veiled this servitude may appear.

What was in simple truth vouchsafed to the Israelites—which they took in and guarded in a childlike way—appeared among other peoples through mixed, impure revelations in horrible, fumbling imitation of the truly holy. The Incarnation of the Word from God through a Virgin was so guarded [a secret] that only the holiest among the Jews, through inner illumination, acknowledged it, whereas the others had the Redeemer killed. Other peoples did have vague traditions of God becoming a human being, and on this account performed hideous, lecherous sacred rituals in worship of the sexual symbols of their mysteries.

So also were the Egyptians—whose skill with dream visions and soothsaying were of the highest order—well aware of the holiness of Joseph and Asenath in the world-historic significance of their conjugal relationship. But as in all things, their understanding was dull and clouded, so that their striving was to keep hold of the remains of the two while crushing the Israelites, hoping, so to say, to themselves swallow whole the Holy Thing of humankind. For all peoples at that time strove and struggled to be the people of the Promise—indeed, it was just in this way that the mystery was veiled.

These few intimations must suffice, for it is not possible for all people to comprehend such things in full, or to express them in all their purity—and this precisely because by virtue of the fall into sin each participates to some degree in the spread of darkness and impurity.

Moses
(Including Aaron, Segola, Jethro, Sephorah, and Separate Articles on Malachi, Spy of Moses, and Rahab)

I HAVE always seen Moses represented as a tall, broad-shoul-dered man. He had a high, somewhat pyramidal head, a large hooked nose, and upon his broad, high forehead were two bumps inclining toward each other and giving him a very remarkable appearance. In his childhood they were like little warts. His complexion was brown, bright and ruddy, his hair inclined to red. I saw many such protuberances as those possessed by Moses on the foreheads of the ancient prophets and hermits; sometimes only one such excrescence appeared upon the middle of the forehead.[1]

Now, as was said before, at the time when Jacob was nearing death, and Joseph was by his side, Jacob put his feet from the couch to the floor, and Joseph had to lay his hand under his father's hip and swear to bury him in Canaan. While Joseph swore, Jacob adored the Blessing hidden in him, for he knew that Joseph had received from an angel the Blessing that had been withdrawn from himself. Joseph bore this Blessing in his right side

---

[1] On another occasion Anne Catherine says: "In a picture I saw Moses dressed in a flowing praying-mantle like the one he wore when he went up the mountain to ask something of God; he was not holding the tablets of the law in his hand—they were hanging at his side or on his arm. Moses was very tall and broad-shouldered. He had red hair. His head was very long and pointed, like a sugarloaf, and he had a big hooked nose. On his broad forehead he had two protuberances like horns, turned inwards towards each other. They were not hard like animals' horns, but had soft skin, as it were ribbed or streaked, and only projected slightly from the forehead like two small lumps, brownish and wrinkled. He already had them as a child, but then they were little warts. This gave him a very strange appearance, which I never liked because it reminded me involuntarily of pictures of satan. I have several times seen protuberances like these on the foreheads of old prophets and of some old hermits. Some of these had only one, in the middle of the forehead." Elsewhere we find this brief note: "Moses was a seer from his cradle, but he saw according to God, and he always practiced what he saw."

21

until death. Even after death it lay enclosed in his body until the
night before the departure of the Israelites, when Moses took
possession of it and placed it in the Ark of the Covenant, together
with the remains of Joseph, as the Sacred Thing of the chosen
people. The Jewish people at large knew only of Joseph's corpse,
but not of the Mystery it contained—that was known to only a
few. But the entire nation grieved deeply when the ancients found
out and made known to them that the Holy Thing upon which
the Promise rested had been stolen. Then Moses, who had been
reared at Pharaoh's court in all the Egyptian wisdom, visited his
people and learned the cause of their grief.[1]

When Moses murdered the Egyptian, God ordained that, as a
fugitive, he should go to Jethro,[2] since the latter, by his connection with the prophetess Segola,[3] would be able to help him discover the purloined Mystery.[4] God led Moses to Jethro also in
order to marry his daughter Sephora,[5] because there was holy
substance in her that had to be gathered to Israel.[6]

---

[1] "Moses wielded much authority in Pharaoh's court. On one occasion,
during a war, he was sent with some soldiers to a marshy region. He was at
this time already most wise and much favored by God. There he and his com-
pany were plagued by flying serpents, all of which, through his supplications,
tumbled to their death into a morass. These creatures were brown upon their
backs, and upon their bellies white."

[2] Jethro lived in the land of the Midianites, northeast of Sinai.

[3] Anne Catherine did not indicate whether Jethro was related to Segola,
or—as tradition has it—was himself at one time in the palace of the Pharaoh,
or even initiated into the mysteries of the children of Israel as a descendent of
Abraham through Keturah. Elsewhere Anne Catherine summarized simply,
saying that Segola, the Egyptian prophetess, was she who handed on to Moses
the corporal mystery of Joseph and Asenath—to which Brentano appended:
"Perhaps she transposed the name Suleica to the name Segola, for the former
appears in the traditional accounts of Joseph and Moses in Egypt." In some
rabbinic and Muslim traditions a woman named Suleica, or Zuleika, is said to
have been one of the chief wives of Potiphar.

[4] See the latter part of "Joseph and Asenath."

[5] Sephora, or Zipporah, was one of the seven daughters of Jethro.

[6] Brentano wrote down in a extensive remark the results of his further
research: "A special light is cast on the stay of Moses with Jethro, and on God's
subsequent command that Moses lead his people out of Egypt thereafter,

Segola was the natural daughter of Pharaoh by a Jewish mother. Although reared in the Egyptian star worship, she was very fond of the Jews. It was she who had divulged to Moses while still at court that he was not a son of Pharaoh.[1]

[Moses's brother] Aaron, after the death of his first wife, had to marry a daughter of this Segola, in order that the mother's influence with the Israelites might be increased. The children of this marriage went with the Israelites at their departure from Egypt. But Aaron was obliged to separate from his wife and marry Elizabeth, the daughter of Aminadab, in order that the Aaronic priesthood might spring from a purely Jewish stock. One of Aaron's sons died in the wilderness in a battle with this tribe. This daughter of Segola, after her separation from Aaron, married again. Her descendants at the time of Christ Jesus dwelt at Abila, whither her mummy had been brought by them. It was through her connection with Jethro that she was brought there.

Segola Presents Moses with the Mystery

ON the night upon which the Angel of the Lord struck the firstborn of the Egyptians,[2] Segola, wrapped in her veil, accompanied Moses, Aaron, and three other Israelites to two sepulchral mounds

---

when we connect Anne Catherine's remark that Jethro led Moses on the track of the Mystery that had been hidden by the Egyptians with the following rabbinical tradition: In his orchard Jethro had a miraculous sapphire root that God had created on the sixth day and put into the hands of Adam. From him it had been passed on to Noah, Abraham, Isaac, Jacob, and then to Joseph, who ruled over Egypt. From him it came to the Pharaoh, and then into the hands of Jethro, who was his counselor. Because Jethro defended the Israelites and their wellbeing against Balaam, he was banished from the court. He planted the root in his garden, but nobody could pull it out, also not he himself, until Moses did so, thereby winning the hand of his daughter [Sephorah] in marriage." (*Fabricii Codex pseudepigraphicus Veteris Testamenti*, p. 806)

[1] "Segola was very enlightened and possessed great influence over Pharaoh. She had on her forehead a bump such as many of the prophets had in olden times. She was led by the Spirit to procure numerous favors and gifts for the Israelites."

[2] That is, the first Passover.

—neither of which offered an obvious entrance—that were separated by a canal over which lay a bridge. The canal flowed between Memphis and Goshen into the Nile. The sepulchral mounds lay on either side of the canal, as I said, and it seems to me that something must remain of them to this day. (Anne Catherine described five [later saying instead "several"] raised places upon one of the mounds—see diagram.)

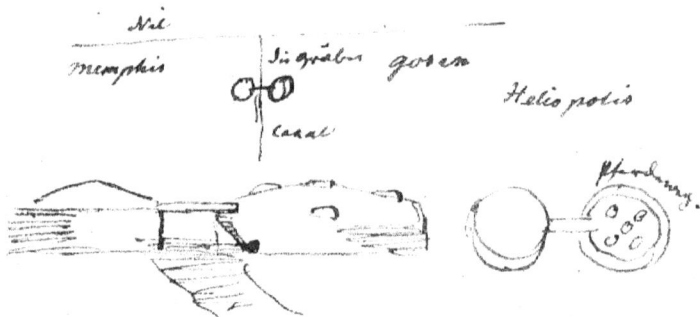

The entrance into the mounds [as it turned out] was under the bridge and below the surface of the water.[1] Steps led from the bridge down to it. Segola descended alone with Moses. She cast into the water a scrap of paper inscribed with the Name of God, following which the water retreated and left the entrance to the monument free. They stepped down and struck on the stone door, which opened inward. Then they pounded on the bridge,

---

[1] In the margin Brentano wrote some notes regarding research he pursued in an effort to establish a further basis for what was recounted in the vision, as follows: "In Gaulmain's *Rabbinensage* and *Vita Moysis* we read that, on the advice of his mage, Pharaoh arranged that the body of Joseph, laden further with the weight of 500 talents, be sunk into the mire of the Nile, over which an irrigation canal was then constructed. Later, it would take a miracle for Moses to rediscover this site (Baumgarten, *Allgemeine Welthistorie*, II, p. 347). Also, according to the Muslims, the corpse of Joseph was interred in the bed of the Nile (ibid., p. 350); and we read further that the Egyptians undertook to sink Joseph's corpse into the Nile as a stratagem to ward off famine (ibid.). An older woman disclosed to Moses the corpse, which through prayer he raised out of its watery grave (ibid., p. 409, k)."

calling the other four to come down. When they did so, Moses bound their hands together with his stole and made them swear a solemn oath to protect the Mystery. After the oath, he loosed their hands and all entered the vault, where they struck a light that revealed all kinds of passages with images of the dead standing therein.

Joseph's body, with the remains of Asenath, lay in an Egyptian tauriform, metal coffin, which shone like polished gold. It had a small head and horns, and between the latter a short staff surmounted with a little crown or headpiece.[1] And it bore symbols on either side.[2] The back formed a cover. This they lifted off, and there lay the hollow body of Joseph, wrapped in cloths.

There was an incision in the side of the body [Anne Catherine twice used the expression *Bauchklappe*, or "belly flap"]. Several ribs were missing, and the heart and vascular system were wrapped in what appeared to be weavings of cotton. The holy Mystery, however, lay in the hollow corpse: it was the uterus of Asenath, slit at the seam so that the holy generative organ of Joseph could be laid therein—all was still in place as it had been left so long ago. The remains of this organ were not laid opposite that of Asenath, but rather, the vascular remains of the Blessing of Joseph were ranged alongside the ovaries of Asenath. To better express the significance of this arrangement one might speak of a *oneness*, rather than a *uniting*, of the two sexes. In form the Mystery was rather like a pear, ribbed, and extensible. It was wrapped in cloth. Segola recovered it, then carried it in her arms concealed under her garments.[3]

The remaining members of Joseph's corpse were placed together upon a stone, wrapped in smaller portions, and carried away by the men. Moses however took with him the image of the small crown or headpiece set between the horns of the tauriform figure. Now that they had gained possession of the Sacred Thing,

---

[1] Here Brentano added as a note the word "phallus."

[2] Brentano later added (from ibid., p. 434): "Some are of the opinion that Isis placed the members of Osiris, who had been murdered by Typhon, in a wooden cow, which she then covered with a linen cloth."

[3] Anne Catherine used the expression "in her apron."

Israel could depart from the country. Segola wept, but Israel was full of joy.

Afterward, Moses concealed a relic of Joseph's body in the top of his staff. This top was in form like a medlar, or persimmon; it was yellowish and surrounded by leaves.[1] It was different from the shepherd's staff that Moses was commanded to cast on the ground before God, and which was then changed into a serpent. It was a reed: the upper and the lower ends could be pushed in and drawn out. With the lower point, which appeared to be of metal and was in form like a sharp pencil, Moses touched the rock as if tracing words upon it. The rock opened under the point, and water gushed forth. Water flowed also from the sand wherever Moses made signs upon it with this staff; the waters of the Red Sea opened before the Holy Thing in the staff of Moses, and the bitter water turned sweet. The Mystery and its Blessing sometimes waned, but then waxed again when, for holy purposes, it was dipped in water [from which people could drink]. From Joseph's death to the departure of Israel from Egypt there were about one hundred and seventy years according to our manner of reckoning. But they had at that time another way of reckoning, other weeks and years. This was often explained to me, but I cannot now recall it. While the Israelites lived in Egypt, they had no temple, but only tents. They piled up stones, poured oil over them, sacrificed grain and lambs, sang, and prayed.

Anne Catherine thought that there was something of the mystery of the Ark of the Covenant in Aaron's staff also:

There was something of a plant-like nature to the staff of Moses, whereas that of Aaron had a more fleshly power.[2] The

---

[1] Anne Catherine adds: "This staff was a mystery possessed from the very beginning by the patriarchs, who passed it on, one to the next. Without this mystery the Israelites could not have come out from Egypt, nor crossed over the Red Sea, whose waters divided before it. This it was that the children of Israel followed on the night it came into the keeping of Moses."

[2] In a note, Brentano here writes: "A transposition seems to have occurred here, because later on Anne Catherine speaks of the greening of Aaron's staff, from which sprout numerous branches with long leaves, whereas the leaves at the tip of the staff of Moses are like those of the beech. She speaks of a green blossoming in water, etc."

mystery of the root in the staff of Moses[1] was transmitted in the giving of the Blessing. This is why Esau was so envious that Jacob received the Blessing. Jacob passed it on to Joseph or his sons. While they were still in Egypt, the children of Israel had drunk from water in which the Holy Thing had been immersed.[2]

It must be so, that at that time the devil had a different, a more corporeal, power at his disposal, for—especially in Egypt—magical operations seemed to arise from out of the earth. I beheld

---

[1] Possibly the sapphire root, once given by God to Adam, and pulled out by Moses in the garden of Jethro (see earlier note by Brentano). Various kabbalistic legends surround the sapphire root, or staff, said to have been given to Adam and Eve by the archangel Raziel when they left the garden of Eden. It was adorned with ten descending sapphire jewels, representing the ten emanations from the Tree of Life, which stands at the heart of Eden. The ten sapphires on the staff (called the ten sephiroth, in connection with the Tree of Life) are said to contain the mystical teaching for reconnecting with the divine, so that when Adam and Eve ventured forth from Eden they carried with them in the form of the sapphire staff a representation of the Tree of Life, and hence of the sephiroth. The sapphire staff was then passed down through the generations, first down to Abraham, and then to Isaac, to Jacob, and to Joseph, then chief advisor of Pharaoh. When Joseph died in Egypt, legend says the staff was taken into the Egyptian palace, and generations later taken by Jethro, priest of Midian. It is said that as Jethro was out walking in his garden one day he plunged the staff into the ground, and when he tried to pull it out, discovered it had taken root and was blossoming. Thereafter none could uproot the staff, which was now become a tree. It was said that the one who could pull it out would not only receive Jethro's daughter Sephorah in marriage but be also redeemer of Israel. And so, the story goes, Moses, who was in the line of Abraham, came to the land of Jethro, and while there grew eager to wed Sephorah. He was therefore challenged to go into Jethro's garden and uproot the tree, an ordeal that had led some who had attempted the feat, and failed, to be devoured by the tree. Moses went to the tree and easily removed it from the ground, thus winning Sephorah's hand, reclaiming the great staff of knowledge, and taking up thereby his destiny as redeemer of Israel. Moses had this staff with him when he encountered the burning thornbush and received his calling to bring Israel out of Egypt. When he wondered how he could achieve this, God ordered that he cast the staff upon the ground, whereupon it became a serpent. Then he was commanded to take the serpent by the tail, and when he did, it became again the staff, imbued with divine powers, with a further destiny in the life of Moses, and in succeeding generations.

[2] Regarding a mystery connected with drinking of water into which had

(though I do not think the magicians themselves did) all manner of horrid animal-like forms rise up from the earth, surround the conjurers, and then pass into them through their mouths like a dark mist. Thereafter they fell into a state of intoxication that seemed to open up to them a capacity to comprehend many things—as though each such animal-like spirit, once swallowed, unsealed within the magician a hitherto entirely self-enclosed world, enabling them then to behold those portions of the earth and its peoples (as well as more remote and hidden things) that bore any relation to that spirit. But magical operations of more recent times seem to me a delusion that increasingly derives from spirits of the air. When I looked behind such spirits, it was like seeing a shadow, or looking behind a door.

Moses and the Ark of the Covenant

ON the same night that Moses took possession of the Holy Thing, a golden casket shaped like a coffin was prepared in which to bear it. It must have been large enough for a man to rest in it, for it was to become a Church, a Body. This was the night upon which the door posts were signed with blood. As I witnessed the rapid working at the chest I thought of the holy cross which, too, was hurriedly put together on the night before the death of Jesus. The chest was of gold plate and shaped like an Egyptian mummi-form coffin, broad above and narrow below. On the upper part was a picture of a face surrounded by beams. On the sides were marked the length of the arms and the position of the ribs. In the center of this coffin-like chest was placed a little golden casket wherein was contained the Holy Thing that Segola had taken out of the sepulchral vault. In the lower part of the chest were sacred vessels, among them the chalice and cups of the patriarchs that Abraham had received from Melchizedek and which with the Blessing had been entailed upon the firstborn. This was the first form of the Ark of the Covenant, and these its first contents.

I saw the Mystery, the Holy Thing, in a form—in a kind of

been immersed for a time the Holy Thing, or some portion thereof, here referred to, see "Joseph and Asenath."

veil—as a substance, as an essence, as strength. It was bread and wine, flesh and blood; it was the Germ of the Blessing before the fall. It was the sacramental presence of that holy propagation of humankind before the fall. It was preserved to humankind by religion. It was possible for it to be ever more and more realized in subsequent generations by a continuous purification through piety, which purification was perfected in Mary, thus rendering her fit to receive, through the Holy Spirit, the long-awaited messiah. Noah, in planting the vineyard, had made the preparation; but here in the Holy Thing were contained already the reconciliation and protection. Abraham had received it in that Blessing which I saw bestowed upon him as something tangible, as a substance. It was a mystery entrusted to one family, therefore the great prerogative of the firstborn.

Before the departure from Egypt, Moses took possession of the Holy Thing. As before this it had been the religious mystery of one family, so now it became the mystery of the whole nation. It was placed in the Ark of the Covenant as the most holy sacrament in the tabernacle and in the monstrance.

When later the children of Israel worshipped the golden calf and fell into gross errors, Moses doubted the power of the Holy Thing. For this he was punished by not being allowed to enter into the promised land. When the Ark fell into the hands of the enemy, the Holy Thing, the bond of union among the Israelites, was removed by the high priest, as was always done when danger threatened. And yet was the Ark still so sacred that the enemy, under the pressure of God's chastising anger, was forced to restore it.

Few comprehended the Holy Thing or the influence it exerted. It often happened that one man by his sins could interrupt the stream of grace, could break the direct genealogical line that was to end in the Savior—or rather in that pure vessel that was to receive him from God. In this way was the redemption of the human race long delayed. But penance could again restore continuity to that line. I do not know for certain whether this sacrament was in itself divine, whether it came forth simply and purely as what it was directly from God, or whether it owed its sacred character to a kind of priestly, supernatural consecration. I think however that the first proposition is the true one, for I know for certain that priests often opposed its action and thus retarded redemption. But they were heavily punished for it, yes, oftentimes even with death itself. When the Holy Thing operated, when prayer was heard, it became bright and increased in size, shining through the cover with a reddish glow. The Blessing proceeding from it increased and diminished at different times according to the purity and piety of humankind. By prayer, sacrifice, and penance, it appeared to grow larger.

I saw Moses expose it before the people only twice: at the passage through the Red Sea and at the worshipping of the golden calf; but even then it was covered. It was removed from the golden casket and veiled, as is the blessed sacrament on Good Friday. Like it, it was carried before the breast or raised up for a blessing or a malediction as if exerting its influence even at a distance. By it, Moses restrained many of the Israelites from idolatry and saved them from death.[1]

A Vision of the Passage of the Red Sea

THE Israelites were encamped on a very low strip of land, about an hour long, on the shore of the Red Sea, which was here very wide. In it were several islands of half an hour in length and from seven to fifteen minutes in breadth. Pharaoh and his army at first sought the Israelites further up the shore, and found them at last

---

[1] A great deal more is to be found in Anne Catherine's visions regarding the Ark of the Covenant (of which there were in fact four, the last being the Virgin Mary), so in the present selection on Moses this brief summary in her own words must suffice: "The ancient Ark of the Covenant, hidden by Jeremiah on Mount Sinai, was never again discovered. The second one was not so beautiful as the first, and it did not contain so many precious things. Aaron's rod was in possession of the Essenes on Horeb, where also a part of the Holy Thing was preserved. The family that Moses appointed as the immediate protectors of the Ark of the Covenant existed till the time of Herod. All will come to light on the last day. Then will the mystery become clear, to the terror of all that have made a bad use of it." For a fuller compilation see "The Ark of the Covenant and the Mystery of the Promise" below and "The Promise of the Redeemer" in *First Beginnings*.

through information given by their scouts. The king thought they would easily fall into his hands, flanked as they were by the sea. The Egyptians were very much incensed against them on account of their carrying off with them their sacred vessels, many of their idols, and the mysteries of their religion.

When the Israelites became aware of the approach of the Egyptians, they were terror-stricken. But Moses prayed and bade them trust in God and follow him. At that moment the pillar of cloud arose behind the Israelites, making so dense a veil that the Egyptians entirely lost sight of them. Then Moses stepped to the shore with his staff (which was forked at the bottom and had a knob on the upper end), prayed, and struck the water. Then appeared before each wing of the army, right and left—as if springing out of the sea—two great luminous pillars, which increased in brilliancy toward the top and terminated in a tongue of flame. At the same time a strong wind parted the waters along the whole of the army (it was about an hour broad) and Moses proceeded along a gently inclining declivity down to the bed of the sea. The whole army followed, at least fifty men abreast. The ground was, at first setting out, somewhat slippery, but soon it became like the softest meadowland, like a mossy carpet. The pillars of fire lit the way before them, and all was as bright as day.

But the most beautiful feature of the whole scene were the islands over which they shed their light. They looked like floating gardens full of the most magnificent fruits and all kinds of animals, which latter the Israelites collected and drove along before them. Without this precaution they would have been in want of food on the other side of the sea. The waters were not divided on either side like perpendicular walls, for they flowed off more in the form of terraces.

The Hebrews went forward with hurrying, sliding steps, balancing themselves like one speeding downhill. It was toward midnight when they entered the bed of the river. The Ark containing Joseph's relics was carried in the center of the fleeing host. The pillars of light rose up out of the water. They appeared to be constantly rotating, and passed not over the islands but around them. At a certain height they were lost in a brilliant luster. The waters did not open all at once, but before Moses's steps, leaving a wedge-formed space until the passage was completed. Near the islands one could see by the light of the pillars the trees and fruits mirrored in the waters.

Another wonderful thing was that the Israelites crossed in three hours, whereas it would have naturally taken nine hours to do so. Higher up the shore, about six to nine hours distant, stood a city that was afterward destroyed by the waters.

At about three o'clock Pharaoh came down to the shore, but was again repulsed by the fog. Soon however he discovered the ford and rolled down into it with his magnificent war chariot, after which hurried his entire army. And now Moses, already on the opposite shore, commanded the waters to return to their original position. Then, the fog and the fire uniting to blind and perplex the Egyptians, all perished miserably in the waves.

Next morning, upon beholding their deliverance, the Israelites chanted the praises of God. On the opposite shore, the two pillars of light united again into one of fire. I cannot do justice to the beauty of this vision.

Moses and the Burning Thornbush

LOOKING out from an altar into the heights I beheld in vision the site where God appeared to Moses in the thornbush. It was a mountainous setting, above and behind a chapel. Stairs mounted up to it on both sides, and there was evidence of a former garden thereabouts. This was where I saw the thornbush. I saw the forty-year-old Moses close by, anxiously hurrying to his flocks. Held back by God's mandate, he had to remove his shoes.

At this juncture, the pilgrim asked Anne Catherine about the appearance of the thornbush, and because it was easiest for her to work with the paper she used for sewing patterns, she asked for some, then proceeded to cut out an outline of the thornbush. When she had completed the attached image on the paper, she said:

It was like an arbor or lattice, deeper than it was tall, of a height such that a child might enter it, or a man lie within. In form it was as though the chalice used at the Last Supper were lying on its side, somewhat flattened below, like a fish-trap. The thorns were matted together like felt, and the surface quite

The Golden Calf

Moses Destroys the Tablets of the Ten Commandments

smooth, covered with narrow leaves about a finger wide, as well as numerous small, light, violet-blue blossoms. Larger twigs hung down on the inside. It looked to me as though a small, radiant figure descended into it and stood there with extended arms, blazing out with reddish fire through the twigs.

I saw also that upon this spot a mystery was later established, to do with the Holy Virgin in connection with her ancestors, but I have forgotten what this was.

I saw the highest peak of Sinai, where God alone was when He was speaking to Moses, surrounded by fire; Moses himself was at a lower level, where was a cleft in the mountain in which, full of fear, he hid himself. I also saw an image imprinted in the mountain of a man fleeing forward, arms outstretched in fear, head hung to one side in anxiety. He was fleeing in a soft mass, making room within. It was a large shape. In the vicinity is a well that Moses called forth.

The Tablets of Moses

THE tablets of Moses were thin and white. God wrote with His finger upon a cloud, and Moses copied down what was there written. The lines were impressed into one side of the tablet, and expressed on the other. The impressions were filled in with gold. When Moses threw down the tablets, one was shattered. The second was thicker. They had been fabricated by a stone-mason at the foot of the mountain.

The Golden Calf

THE golden calf worshipped in the wilderness by the children of Israel was comprised of two sections screwed together, and its head was massive. It was like a yearling cow. It was finely wrought, its neck bent slightly backward. It had small horns and a white starlet raised up nobly on the front of its head, and on its chest was a yellow flag star. It stood tall, its thin body borne upon slender legs.

At this point the pilgrim adds: The golden calf, which Aaron had cast from the jewelry of the Israelites—and to which they prayed, saying "That is your god, who led you out of Egypt"—signifies that in place of the Holy Thing, Aaron employed as a surrogate the Egyptian tauriform coffin in which the Mystery was kept. Moses may have taken the Holy Thing with him to the mountain, and neither before nor after this time were the people cognizant of it as an object of worship. And so, since the people had no longer a central object of worship and did not know when Moses would come back, Aaron gave in to their pressing demands and presented them with the Egyptian symbol of the mystery. Moses burned the calf to powder, which he mixed with water and gave the idolaters to drink.[1]

Moses and Mary

AT the time of the journey of the child Mary to the Temple I saw also two boys present. They were not human. They appeared there supernaturally and with a spiritual signification. They carried long standards rolled upon staffs furnished with knobs at both ends. The larger of the two boys came to me with his standard unfurled, read, and explained it to me. The writing appeared entirely strange to me, the single, golden letters all inverted. One letter represented a whole word. The language sounded unfamil-

---

[1] Regarding this, some rabbis say that the effect of drinking the "passion-water" (*Eiferwasser*, water used in cases of *Eifersucht*, that is, jealousy) was that those in a state of guilt would swell up and become lame (see *Allgemeine Welt-historie*, II, p. 442, note (# H). Perhaps Moses had immersed the Mystery in

iar, but I understood it all the same. He showed me in his roll the passage referring to the burning thornbush of Moses. He explained to me how the thornbush burned and yet was not consumed; so now was the child Mary inflamed with the fire of the Holy Spirit, but in her humility knew nothing of it. It signifies also the divinity and humanity in Jesus, and how God's fire united with the child Mary.

Later, at the time of Mary's visitation, I saw Mary and Elizabeth reciting together, morning and evening, the hymn of thanksgiving, the *Magnificat*, which Mary had received from the Holy Spirit at the salutation of Elizabeth. At the second part, which refers to God's Promise, I saw the previous history of the most holy Incarnation and the Mystery of the most holy sacrament of the altar, from Abraham down to Mary. I saw Abraham sacrificing Isaac, also the Mystery of the Ark of the Covenant, which, as has been said, Moses received on the night before the departure from Egypt, and by which he was enabled to escape and conquer. I recognized its connection with the holy incarna-

---

water. The expression "become lame" is reminiscent of Jacob's being lamed as the angel took from him the Mystery. Anne Catherine says further: "This water (*Eiferwasser*), by means of which women accused of infidelity to their husbands were put to the test, was such that the Mystery had first been dipped into it. Should a woman prove guilty, her body would rupture. But such a water into which the Mystery had been immersed could be drunk also as a blessing. Such a blessing was imbibed by three holy women: the prophetess Deborah; Hanna of Shiloh, the mother of Samuel; and the mother of holy Anne [the Essene Ismeria, married to Eliud, who had two other daughters: Sobe and Maraha], who took her drink among the Essenes—for in her time they still possessed a part of the Mystery on Mount Carmel. It had come to them when the Temple was destroyed, and I saw it as though surrounded with small, flourishing trees. Anne's mother had already other children before she took the holy draught through which she was prepared to conceive Anne." For more on the subject of such holy water and the mystery of immersion, see "Joseph and Asenath."

"David took such a draught also, after he had done penance before Nathan. Later, because the line of David was in danger of being blotted out, Elisha cried out upon the mountain, 'Lord, I will take to me a wife, if you but give me the holy seed.' Then he was sent to give a draught [of holy water] to a side-branch of the stock of David in the region of Bethlehem. This side-branch then rejoined the line of the messiah."

tion, and it seemed to me as if this mystery were now fulfilled or living in Mary. I saw also the prophet Isaiah and his prophecy of the Virgin, and from him to Mary visions of the approach of the most blessed sacrament.

At the birth of Jesus, when Mary told Joseph that her time was drawing near and that he should now betake himself to prayer, he left her and turned toward his sleeping place to do her bidding. Before entering his little recess he looked back once toward that part of the cave where Mary knelt upon her couch in prayer, her back to him, her face toward the east. He saw the cave filled with the light that streamed from Mary, for she was entirely enveloped as if by flames. It was as if he were, like Moses, looking into the burning bush.

Moses and the Transfiguration

WHAT *follows regarding the appearance of Moses at the Transfiguration on Mount Tabor, occurred on the night of Tuesday/Wednesday, April 3/4, AD 31.*

The apostles (Peter, James the Greater, and John of Zebedee) lay, ravished in ecstasy rather than in sleep, prostrate on their faces. Then I saw three shining figures approaching Jesus in the light. Their coming appeared perfectly natural. It was like that of one who steps from the darkness of night into a place brilliantly illuminated. Two of them appeared in a more definite form, a form more like the corporeal. They addressed Jesus and conversed with him. They were Moses and Elijah. The third apparition spoke no word. It was more ethereal, more spiritual. That was Malachi.

I heard Moses and Elijah greet Jesus, and I heard him speaking to them of his passion and of redemption. Their being together appeared perfectly simple and natural. Moses and Elijah did not look aged nor decrepit as when they left the earth. They were on the contrary in the bloom of youth. Moses—taller, graver, and more majestic than Elijah—had on his forehead something like two projecting bumps. He was clothed in a long garment. He looked like a resolute man, like one who could govern with strictness, though at the same time he bore the impress of purity, rectitude, and simplicity. He told Jesus how rejoiced he was to see him who had led himself and his people out of Egypt, and who was now once more about to redeem them. He referred to the numerous types of the Savior in his own time, and uttered deeply significant words upon the Paschal lamb and the lamb of God.

Elijah was quite the opposite of Moses. He appeared to be more refined, more lovable, of a sweeter disposition. But both Elijah and Moses were very dissimilar from the apparition of Malachi, for in the former one could trace something human, something earthly in form and countenance; yes, there was even a family likeness between them. Malachi, however, looked quite different. There was in his appearance something supernatural. He looked like an angel, like the personification of strength and repose. He was more tranquil, more spiritual than the others.

Jesus spoke with them of all the sufferings he had endured up to the present, and of all that still awaited him. He related the history of his passion in detail, point by point. Elijah and Moses frequently expressed their emotion and joy. Their words were full of sympathy and consolation, of reverence for the Savior, and of the uninterrupted praises of God. They constantly referred to the types of the mysteries of which Jesus was speaking, and praised God for having from all eternity dealt in mercy toward his people. But Malachi kept silence.

The disciples raised their heads, gazed long upon the glory of Jesus, and beheld Moses, Elijah, and Malachi. When in describing his passion Jesus came to his exaltation on the cross, he extended his arms at the words: "So shall the Son of Man be lifted up!" His face was turned toward the south, he was entirely penetrated with light, and his robe flashed with a bluish white gleam. He, the prophets, and the three apostles—all were raised above the earth.

And now the prophets separated from Jesus, Elijah and Moses vanishing toward the east, Malachi westward into the darkness. Then Peter, ravished with joy, exclaimed: "Master, it is good for us to be here! Let us make here three tabernacles: one for thee, one for Moses, and one for Elijah!" Peter meant that they had need of no other heaven, for where they were was so sweet and blessed. By the tabernacles he meant places of rest and honor, the dwellings of the saints. He said this in the delirium of his joy, in his state of ecstasy, without knowing what he was saying.

✛ ✛ ✛ ✛ ✛

ON Sunday, September 11, AD 29, Jesus and Eliud arrived back at Eliud's home in the early hours of the morning. Jesus's disciples, a number of Essenes, and some other people—including two Pharisees from Nazareth—gathered together to hear his discourses. The Pharisees invited Jesus to come to them and later conducted him to the synagogue. There he taught concerning Moses and the prophecies of the coming of the messiah.

On Friday, October 7, AD 29, in the city Gilgal, I saw Jesus enter the precincts of a sacred spot open to prophets and doctors of the law. On this occasion I saw the death of Moses, which took place upon a low, but steep peak of Mount Nebo, which rises between Arabia and Moab. The camp of the Israelites flanked the mount, the outposts extending far into the valley around. A growth like ivy covered the whole mount. It was short and crisp, and grew in tufts like the juniper. Moses was obliged to support himself by it when climbing to the top of the peak. Joshua and Eliezer were with him. Moses had a vision from God, which his companions saw not. He delivered to Joshua a roll of writing containing six maledictions and six benedictions, which the latter had to publish to the people when in the promised land. Then, having embraced them, he commanded them to depart and not to look back. When they had gone Moses cast himself upon his knees with outstretched arms and gently sank upon his side dead. I saw the earth open under him and enclose him as in a beautiful grave. When Moses appeared at the Transfiguration of Jesus on Tabor, I saw that he came from that place. Joshua read the six blessings and six maledictions before the people.

On the morning of Thursday, September 7, AD 30, Jesus gave a discourse in the non-Jewish quarter of Ainon, speaking at length of Moses in the wilderness on Mounts Sinai and Horeb, of the construction of the Ark of the Covenant, of the table of showbread, etc. As the ancestors of his hearers had sent offerings for the same, Jesus alluded to them as symbolical. He exhorted them now, in the time of their fulfillment, to bring heart and soul as an offering by penance and conversion, and he showed them the connection between that offering of their forefathers and their own present condition. I do not remember it all, but the substance of this discourse was as follows: While Jesus was speaking, I had an extended and circumstantial vision of the Exodus of the Israelites from Egypt. I saw that Jethro, the father-in-law, and Sephora, the wife of Moses, dwelt in Arga with the two sons and a daughter of the latter. I saw Jethro with the wife and children of Moses journeying to join him on Mount Horeb. Moses received them most joyfully and related all the miracles wrought by God for the deliverance of his people from Egypt, whereupon Jethro offered sacrifice. I saw too that Moses at this time settled the disputes of all the Israelites himself, but Jethro counseled him to nominate subordinate judges. He then returned home, leaving Sephora and her sons with Moses. I saw Jethro recounting in Arga all the wonders he had seen, and many were thereby roused to great reverence for the God of the Israelites. Then Jethro sent Moses presents and offerings on camels, to which the Argites had contributed. The presents consisted of fine oil, which was afterward burned before the tabernacle; very fine, long strands of camel's hair for spinning and weaving into covers and curtains; and most beautiful setim wood, which was afterward made into the poles of the Ark of the Covenant and the table for the showbread.

On the morning of Monday, September 18, AD 30, after healing many people and teaching in the synagogue of Betharamphtha, Jesus and his disciples then proceeded to Abila, where he taught at an open place where there was a pillar erected in memory of Elijah. On the declivity of the mountain west of the city of Abila I saw a very beautiful sepulcher in front of which was a little garden. In the latter were assembled the women belonging to three families of Abila. They were celebrating a solemnity in honor of the dead. They sat on the ground closely veiled, wept, uttered lamentations, and frequently prostrated with the face to the earth. They killed several birds of very beautiful plumage, plucked them, and burned the lovely, shining feathers on the tomb. The flesh was afterward given to the poor. The tomb was that of an Egyptian woman from whom the mourners had descended. Before the departure of the children of Israel, there lived in Egypt an illegitimate relative of the Pharaoh then reigning. She was very favorably disposed toward Moses, and rendered great services to the Israelites. She was a prophetess, and she it was that had discovered Joseph's mummy to Moses on the last night of his stay in Egypt. Her name was Segola, and she was the mother of Aaron's wife, from whom however he separated and married Elizabeth, the daughter of Aminadab of the tribe of Judah. The repudiated wife also was connected in some way with Aminadab, but how I do not now know. She had by her mother Segola, as well as by Aaron himself, been richly dowered. Taking with her large treasure, she accompanied the Israelites on their departure and married a second time during their stay in the desert. She afterward attached herself to the Midianites, especially to the family of Jethro. Her descendants settled near Abila, where they dwelt under tents, and it was here that she was buried. After the time of the prophet Elijah, Abila was built, and it was then that those descendants settled there. I did not see the city in Elijah's time; it may have been destroyed before him. There were still three families of those descendants in Abila, and they were celebrating today the anniversary of the death of their ancestress, Segola's daughter, whose mummy had been transported hither from the desert and entombed. The women made an offering of their earrings and other trinkets to the Levites in memory of their deceased relative. Jesus praised her from the pulpit of Elijah and spoke of the goodness of Segola, her mother. The women listened attentively from where they stood behind the men.

On the morning of Saturday, April 28, AD 31, Jesus taught in the synagogue upon sacrifice, taking his texts from the third book of Moses (Leviticus) and the prophet Ezekiel. There was something marvelously sweet and impressive in his words as he showed that the laws of Moses were now realizing their most elevated signification. He spoke of the offering of a pure heart. He said that sacrifices multiplied a thousand times could no more be of any avail, for one must purify his soul and offer his passions as a holocaust. Without rejecting anything, without condemning or abolishing any of the prescriptions of the Mosaic law, he explained it according to its real signification, thus making it appear far more beautiful and worthy of reverence.

On Sunday, May 13, AD 31, Jesus taught at the place of baptism. Seven bridal couples were present. Jesus gave them instruction concerning marriage. Among the bridegrooms two were converted pagans who had received circumcision and espoused Jewish maidens. There were some other pagans inclined toward Judaism, who had sought and obtained permission to assist at the instructions with them. After citing other instances involving pagans, Jesus alluded to Segola, that pious pagan woman of Egypt who settled at Abila and performed so many good works that she at last found favor in the sight of God. Then he showed them how the pagans ought to strive to practice virtue, that thereby they might attract upon themselves divine grace, for his pagan listeners knew something of Elijah and Segola.

At the time of the Last Passover, the slaughter of the lamb for Jesus and the apostles presented a scene most touching. It took place in the anteroom of the cenacle, Simeon's son, the Levite, assisting at it. The apostles and disciples were present chanting the 118th Psalm. Jesus spoke of a new period then beginning, and said that the sacrifice of Moses and the signification of the Paschal lamb were about to be fulfilled, that on this account the lamb was to be immolated as formerly in Egypt, and that now in reality were they to go forth from the house of bondage.

On Holy Saturday, in the course of his descent into hell, the Lord turned to the circle on the right, to limbo proper. There he met the soul of the good thief [Dismas] going under the escort of angels into Abraham's bosom, while the bad thief [Gesmas], encompassed by demons, was being dragged down into hell. The soul of Jesus addressed some words to both, and then, accompanied by a multitude of angels, of the redeemed, and by those demons that were driven out of the first circle, went likewise into the bosom of Abraham. This space, or circle, appeared to me to lie higher than the other. It was as if a person climbed from the earth under the churchyard up into the church itself. The evil spirits struggled in their chains and wanted not to enter, but the angels forced them on. In this second circle were all the holy Israelites to the left, the patriarchs, Moses, the Judges, the Kings; on the right, the prophets and all the ancestors of Jesus, as also his relatives down to Joachim, Anne, Joseph, Zechariah, Elizabeth, and John. There were no demons in this circle, no pain nor torment, only the ardent longing for the fulfillment of the Promise now realized.

Malachi the Spy of Moses

ON Wednesday. September 27, AD 30, Jesus went with twelve disciples five hours to the south [of Dion] and over the brook that flowed down from the valley of Ephron. One half-hour to the south of this brook lay Jogbeha, a little, unknown place, quite hidden away in a hollow behind a forest. It was founded by a prophet, a spy of Moses and Jethro, whose name sounds like Malachi. He is not, however, one and the same with the last prophet, Malachi. Jethro, the father-in-law of Moses, employed [this other] Malachi as a servant. He was exceedingly faithful and prudent, on which account Moses sent him to explore this country. He had come two years before Moses himself arrived, had explored the country for miles around—even as far as the borders of the lake—and had given an account of all he saw. Jethro at that time dwelt near the Red Sea, but upon Malachi's report he went with the wife and sons of Moses to Arga.

Malachi was at last pursued as a spy. They hunted him to kill him. There was no city here in those times, only a few people living in tents. Malachi took refuge in a swamp, or cistern, and an angel appeared and helped him. He brought him, upon a long strip of parchment, the command to continue three years longer reconnoitering the country. The inhabitants, that is, those who lived in the tents, provided him with clothes such as they themselves wore—long red tunics and jackets of the same color. Malachi also explored the country around Betharamphtha. He lived for some time among the tent-dwellers of Jogbeha, and by his superior intelligence rendered them great assistance.

In the hollow in which Jogbeha was hidden ran a ditch filled with water and quite covered with reeds, and on the spot in which Malachi lay concealed was a well that had been filled up. It began later on to bubble up and cast out quantities of sand with occasional columns of vapor and sometimes pebbles. By degrees was formed around the well a hill, which was soon clothed with verdure. The swamp was filled up by earth brought from a neighboring mountain, and buildings were erected upon it. Thus arose around the well, which was covered by a beautiful springhouse, the city of Jogbeha, which name signifies "It will be elevated." The marshy cistern must have been built around in far earlier times, for lying nearby were the moss-covered ruins of walls in which were still discernible holes intended, most probably, for fish. There were other ruins in this locality rather like the foundation of an ancient tent castle. Malachi taught the inhabitants to use black mineral pitch in building.

On another occasion Anne Catherine reported an extended visionary journey, involving both Malachi the spy of Moses, and Malachi the prophet. What follows is the initial part of that journey:[1]

I had a most difficult night, during which I undertook an arduous journey, for I had to discharge a mission. A thousand obstacles stood in my way: I was pursued, robbers seized upon me, I suffered thirst and hunger, heat, exhaustion, and was chased by evil spirits. But in spite of all I fulfilled my commission, which was to take on the form of Malachi of Jogbeha,[2] who had acted as a spy or scout for Moses,[3] and travel under this guise to a certain man who dwelt upon an African island, in order to convey to him a message. And since this Malachi had resided in Jogbeha, I had to clothe myself as he would have done.

There was something amusing about this, however—as though I were myself descended from this same Malachi. But another spirit accompanied me, the prophet Malachi, who instructed me throughout. And so I journeyed—in great danger and need—through the land of Judea, the wilderness of Sinai, and along Arabia by the Red Sea, which I then crossed over. Along the way I saw everything that had formerly happened there that bore some reference to my mission. I saw also many circumstances in the life of the prophet Malachi himself, and those of other prophets from

---

[1] See "Vision Journey with Malachi" later in this volume.

[2] Identified with a town near Amman, capital of Jordan.

[3] See also "Rahab" immediately below in this article, as her story is connected with that of Joshua, another spy of Moses.

the time of the Babylonian captivity, as well as something of Ezra, holy scripture, and another holy book.[1]

Rahab

I SAW the red threads of the house of Rahab[2] in Jericho as a prefiguration of the redeeming streams of the blood of Jesus. I saw there was something good in this woman, that she had once dreamt of five bloody streams descending from heaven to redeem the world, and that the red threads she was instructed to hang before her house was done according to God's will.[3]

---

[1] See "Ezra and the Canon" and "The Book of Ctesiphon • Zoroaster."

[2] According to Joshua 2:1–7, when the Hebrews were encamped at Shittim, in the "Arabah" or Jordan valley opposite Jericho, ready to cross the river, Joshua, as a final preparation, sent out two spies to investigate the military strength of Jericho. (Joshua himself is known as "one of the twelves spies" sent out by Moses to reconnoiter the land of Canaan—see also "Malachi, Spy of Moses.") The spies stayed in Rahab's house, which was built into the city wall. The soldiers sent to capture the spies asked Rahab to bring them out. (Joshua 2:3). Instead she hid them under bundles of flax on the roof. It was the time of the barley harvest, and flax and barley are ripe at the same time in the Jordan valley, so that "the bundles of flax stalks might have been expected to be drying just then." After escaping, the spies promised to spare Rahab and her family after taking the city, even if there should be a massacre, if she would mark her house by hanging a red cord out the window. When the city of Jericho fell, Rahab and her whole family were preserved according to the promise of the spies, and were incorporated among the Jewish people. In the New Testament, Rahab of the book of Joshua is mentioned as an example of a person of faith (Hebrews 11:31) and good works (James 2:25). Rahab is referred to as "the harlot" in each of these passages. A woman, Rahab, is also mentioned in the Gospel of Matthew as one of the ancestors of Jesus (Matthew 1:5). She married Salmon of the tribe of Judah and was the mother of Boaz. Most other English bibles transcribe her name as Rachab. Some scholars suggest that the two women were not the same, although in Anne Catherine's vision elements of both accounts are narrated as of the same Rahab. Rahab is depicted as a virtuous soul in the third circle of heaven in Dante's *Divine Comedy* (*Paradiso* 9.112 ff.)

[3] Joshua 2:18–21. See also "Samson" below, where Rahab is mentioned as a type also of Thamar (Tamar).

I saw that the procession around the city [of Jericho] with the Ark of the Covenant and trumpets was related to Jesus's journeys.

Anne Catherine said that in the course of the three years of his ministry, she saw Jesus journey five times through the land. However, the Israelites circled seven times around Jericho. It was, however, difficult to understand the things she said on this occasion. On the following day she added that what she had described from her vision the previous day regarding Rahab and five red cords stretching down from heaven—as also the five threads hung before her house—had to do with the accomplishment of God's purpose for her: that through her marriage to Salmon she would enter into the bloodline of Jesus (Matt.1:5). That evening she clarified further, describing that the Israelites circled Jericho seven times, and Christ Jesus traveled five times through the promised land— the fifth journey being the most extensive, as was also the fifth and last of his five wounds. At the end he went to Bethany, whence he traveled seven times to Jerusalem, teaching openly. Each day he returned to the city. The second of these journeys was on Palm Sunday. His last three days he remained in the vicinity of Bethany. He died at the age of thirty-three years and three months.

Samson and Delilah

I BEHELD much of the life of Samson, but owing to my poor health have only been able to retain what follows.

Samson's mother was from the tribe of Judah on her father's side, though her mother—a maiden or slave—was a secondary wife or concubine. She (Samson's mother) was quite beautiful. An angel had announced to her that she would bear Samson, and to that end bid that she and her husband prepare an offering to the Lord, which they did. The angel then offered their offering in turn to a priest, disappearing then in the flames, facing heaven.

Samson was exceptionally handsome, clever, and powerful. Already as a boy his counsel was frequently sought, though at first in jest. But as his great wisdom came more and more to light, he was often called upon to participate in matters of tribal justice; and he offered such thorough and perspicacious opinions in regard to the tribulations suffered at the hands of the Philistines that even when only between the ages of ten and fifteen years he took on the role of Judge. He died in Gaza in his thirty-fifth year. He was good-looking and of great stature, though not excessively large. His manner of dress was pure and noble, finer than that of most, though his armor was not overly splendid and he went about unarmed.

Frequently I saw Samson watching and praying in caves; also, he received divine illuminations. He was feared by the Philistines, although to a certain degree they chose to tolerate him. At God's behest he was to seek out and marry a Philistine woman, and knew already what would in due course follow therefrom. Many of his deeds were like prefigurations of those of Jesus and the Church. I was shown the meaning of such deeds as the ripping apart of the lions, and the honey later found in their jaws, as also his concealing his actions from his parents—but can no longer recall more about these matters.

He wore his long blonde hair in numerous braids wound around his head like a hood and in chignons over his forehead and at the sides, rather like purses. His strength lay not so much in his hair *qua* hair but insofar as it stood testimony to his vow to God. He must have broken his vow wide open when he let this sign of his status as a Nazarite be shaved off.[1]

Samson hid himself in the cave Etham, where for a time he prayed often and lived piously. But the Jews bound him and led him to the Philistines, who, from the neighboring region later called Lechi, sorely oppressed him. There Samson prayed, tore himself free of his bonds, and went forth into a ravine where Philistines were positioned to seize him. But as it happens, animal bones were strewn about, and he seized hold of the jawbone of an ass—a longish bone formed with something like a hook at its anterior end—with which he went to work battering the Philistines, driving them deeper into the ravine. More then set upon him from the rear, aiming to trap him in-between, but he spun around and beat these also deeper down, killing them here and there in grottoes and crevices. The Philistines went dumb from fright and astonishment. Samson appeared then above the ravine,

---

[1] See "Nazarites" immediately following.

gazing with relish at the heap below him, and said triumphantly, "There in piles you lie (there were two groups of attackers); a thousand have I struck dead with the jawbone of an ass."

Perhaps it was because he had first preened himself with self-praise that he was now beset with such thirst that he implored God—who had graced him with such good fortune—not to let him now die parched. Nearby lay a great white round stone that appeared to have separated from the cliff face (where it had previously projected), whether through the action of rain, or simply on account of its enormous weight—creating a kind of gutter off to the side into which he hurled the jawbone. After that, he prayed.

Then Samson noticed that a molar from the jawbone had stuck fast in a chink in the stone, from which small droplets of water were dripping. So he tore the tooth out of the cleft, whereafter the water increased to a trickle and he drank thereof. At a later time the white stone was removed, and beneath where it previously lay is now a lovely spring. The Jews returned to him just as he had discovered the water.

The woman with whom Samson later hid in Gaza was no betrayer. She had fallen into ill fortune. Neither did Samson go to her with a mind to transgression, but in order to arrange for food and lodging while he concealed himself to escape capture in Gaza, where he had something to do. Indeed, he did not actually sin with her; rather did he stay awake in the night and pray. At around midnight, when the watchmen had fallen asleep, he tore out the doors of the city gate and carried them away. This woman was like Thamar,[1] who concealed the spies [of the Israelites] before Jericho.

---

[1] "Thamar" was written in later above this line, but this must be an error; rather should it be "Rahab" (see Joshua 2). CB.

Rahab (or Rachab) was, according to the book of Joshua, a prostitute who lived in Jericho in the promised land and assisted the Israelites in capturing the city. In the New Testament she was lauded as an example of living by faith, while being considered righteous by her works, and was reckoned among the ancestors of Jesus in the Gospel of Matthew. However, the story of Thamar (Tamar) and Judah (Genesis 38) contains related themes. See also "Rahab" above.

Later, Samson made the acquaintance of a woman from Gaza named Delilah. Gaza was situated upon two heights, not far distant from a valley filled with pleasure gardens, greensward, and lovely dwellings. The valley was called Sorek, and it was here that Delilah came together in a summer cottage with Samson. Delilah was not truly a prostitute, but rather a genteel woman divorced from her husband, who did not suit her. She was well-educated, and in Gaza regarded as a prophetess. She was like a priestess as well and had received all sorts of demonic visions. She was very beautiful, strong, uncommonly clever, full of stratagems, and arrogant. In secret she clung to her tribe and its idol worship, but she could also present herself as being entirely friendly to the Jews.

A sort of armed truce had been established at this time between the Philistines and Jews. Samson went back and forth between the two sides. He had known Delilah already for some time, and would often meet her clandestinely. For her part, in order to draw him closer to her, Delilah offered Samson counsel and suggested various schemes. And so, over time, was Samson caught in her snare. Of one thing he was certain: that he took much delight in her cleverness and beauty; and since he could no longer resist her, she led him astray into romantic dalliances. Now, the Philistine princes and priests knew of this affair, and pledged considerable gold and great honor to Delilah if she would but coax from him the secret of how they might overpower him.

Thereafter I saw Samson for a time much in love with Delilah and placing great confidence in her. He had not broken his vow to drink no wine or other intoxicating beverage, but I beheld how through superficial flattery and ceaseless pestering Delilah in due course led him astray in this regard, so that he fell from grace and rushed headlong from one drunken fit to another, falling ever deeper into sin. Through a vile beverage she shook him from his senses, so that he was become like a very animal.

The Philistines, however, after the custom of that time, sought from Samson progeny, whom they might raise up into powerful heros and warriors. With this in view, temple prostitutes were sent to Delilah's domicile, and brought thence to Samson's chamber in the hope that in his drunkenness he would lie with them.

Indeed, some Philistines were stationed next to the chamber to witness which of the prostitutes Samson bedded.

While this atrocity was played out, there occurred a number of futile attempts to bind Samson, which at the same time signified various depravities in which he had entangled himself, and from which he ever and again tore away from himself some portion, until in the end—though falling back ever and again into intoxication and lechery, and not entirely fleeing therefrom—he let it be known that he was a divinely initiated Nazarite, from whom, were he bereft of his long locks (which no shears had yet touched), all strength would ebb.

Delilah told him that she saw now his great love, thus inciting him to ever more drink and sin, bringing him again and again to the other women. But as Samson, now weary of his debauchery, lay as though at death's door on account of his drunkenness and transgressions, Delilah came to him and lay his head upon her lap.

Now, there was a high, broad, long seat along one side of the room, where stood also a number of covered lamps. Delilah held in her hands a most singular shears, like pincers charged with a spring, which one pressed and released with the hand. They resembled sheep shears, and were about the size of an apple.

Delilah unbound Samson's hair and snipped off seven locks thereof. According to what I saw, she did not cut away all his hair, but left, I think, at least the tuft over his forehead. When she called him awake, the Philistines were standing by with cords and chains, and, as Samson was so fatigued (almost in a faint) when he awoke, they fell upon him, cast him in chains, and bored out his eyes with something like a drill. It was gruesome to look upon his bloodied eye sockets while Delilah and the despicable women with whom he had fornicated cursed him, now that he was blind and so, as they thought, posed no threat to them.

And now Samson was set to the most onerous tasks in Gaza. He had to do the milling, trudge great burdens hither and yon, purge the cesspools—into which filth he was himself cast time and again. And all this Samson had to manage without his sight. Yet again they tried to force him to breed with prostitutes, but this he would not do. He was filled with remorse, prayed, and undertook heavy penances. The particular sorts of cords and bonds with which he was tied—and the number thereof—had some associa-tion with women, sexual offences, and wantonness. Finally, exhausted nearly to the point of death, he lost even his status as a Nazarite.

I wept as I beheld Samson's decline into such destitution, and how pitiably he was treated. But as his remorse and penitence grew, so did his strength return with them. Also, the time was now gone by when any of the women with whom he had lay (and who on that account had in the interim been well looked after and protected) could any longer expect to bear a child, so that, as Sam-son could no longer be incited to such liaisons, he was mistreated all the more egregiously.

Then I beheld a great festival of pagan idols. All aristocratic Phi-listines, together with their wives, were assembled in the temple,[1] on all floors. They offered sacrifices, sang and danced, and then had Samson—normally confined in stocks—brought to the festiv-ities. He was placed at the center, where he was misused and almost dragged to death, blind as he was, amid scorn and laugh-ter. They hauled him around, beating him the while, then ran him against the pillars, so that he kept stumbling as he was forced to rush about.

Samson, at an extremity of exhaustion, was now useless as an object of such sport. So the offending youths were instructed to take him beneath the temple to the vault, or cellar. Here he asked to be led to a pillar, that he might rest awhile against it, and sent the lads away. Now did he reflect again upon his wretched-ness, his transgressions, weeping bitterly and beseeching God—and then all his former strength came over him again! He tried to reach the neighboring pillar for purchase but could not extend his arm that far, and so, leaning his body against the one pillar, he planted his staff against the other, and in this way brought down the whole building, which collapsed in upon itself, killing all within.

---

[1] In the manuscript, the word "temple" was stricken out and replaced with "race course," owing to Anne Catherine's more precise account as given in the final paragraph.

I saw Delilah, in a furious rage, tumble from the palace roof into a deep cesspool, crushed to shreds. This woman is indeed more hateful to me than either Herodias or Semiramis.

In fact, it was no temple Samson brought thus crashing down, but a large, round structure composed of one gallery of pillars set upon another, at whose center were played out gladiatorial combats, and where Samson also was hounded nearly to death. It was just when he could bear no more that he was brought down to the cellar, which lay underneath the field of combat. Bracing his back against one column, with his hands he pressed against the others. The edifice [that he thus brought tumbling down] stood in a great racetrack, which itself did not collapse.

Anne Catherine was accustomed, when speaking of persons of historical importance, to explain how they divided their hair. "Eve," she said, "divided her hair in two parts, but Mary into three." And she appeared to attach importance to these words. No opportunity presented itself for her to give any explanation upon the subject, which probably would have shown a deeper meaning in what was done with the hair in sacrifices, funerals, consecrations, or vows, etc. She once said of Samson:

His fair hair, which was long and thick, was gathered up on his head in seven tresses, like a helmet; and the ends of these tresses were fastened upon his forehead and temples. His hair was not in itself the source of his strength, but was so only as having borne witness to the vow he had made to let it grow in God's honor. The powers that depended upon these seven tresses were the seven gifts of the Holy Spirit. He must have already broken his vows and lost many graces by the time he allowed this sign of being a Nazarite to be cut off. I did not see Delilah cut off all his hair, and I think one lock remained on his forehead. But he retained the grace to do penance, and by that repentance he recovered strength sufficient to destroy his enemies. The life of Samson is figurative and prophetic.

✛ ✛ ✛ ✛ ✛

ON Saturday, June 2, AD 31, Jesus went with some Levites to visit Elizabeth's birthplace. Afterward, he went to heal the sick in their homes. While in the city, Jesus went with the Levites to visit and cure the sick of several families. They held out to Jesus their hands enveloped in linen bands. Jesus visited Simeon also in his own house and then proceeded to the synagogue, where he closed the sabbath exercises. Jesus's teaching turned upon sacrifice for sin and upon Samson. He rehearsed the principal deeds of the latter, and spoke of him as of a saint whose life was prophetic. Samson, Jesus said, did not lose all his strength, for he had retained sufficient to do penance. His overturning of the pagan temple upon himself was owing to a special inspiration from God.

On another occasion Anne Catherine said that the shape of a pair of pincers of which she happened to be speaking just then reminded her of the scissors with which Samson's hair had been shorn. In her visions of the third year of the public life of Jesus she had seen the Master keep the sabbath-day at Misael—a town belonging to the Levites, of the tribe of Asher—and as a portion of the book of Judges was read in the synagogue, had beheld the life of Samson.

Nazarites

ON Friday, August 26, AD 29, Jesus went through a pastoral region where later, after the second Passover, he healed a leper. He taught in the different little villages around. But for the sabbath he went with his companions to Jezreel, a scattered place, the houses, which were built in groups, being separated from one another by ruins, towers, and gardens. A highroad ran through the city, called King's street. Jesus had with him only three of his companions, several having gone on before.

Jezreel was the home of strict observers of the Jewish law. They were not Essenes, however, but Nazarites.[1] They made vows for a time, longer or shorter, and practiced various kinds of mortification. They had a large institution, comprising different sections.

---

[1] In the Hebrew bible a Nazirite or Nazarite is one who voluntarily took a vow described in Numbers 6:1–21. "Nazarite" comes from the Hebrew word *Nazir*, meaning "consecrated" or "separated". This vow required the person to: abstain from wine or intoxicating liquors, along with other proscriptions; refrain from cutting the hair on one's head; and not to become ritually impure by contact with corpses or graves, even those of family members. After following these requirements for a designated interval, the person would make three

The unmarried men occupied one part exclusively, the unmarried women another. The married also made vows of continency for a certain period, during which the husbands lived in a house next to that of the unmarried men while the wives retired to that of the single women. They were all clothed in gray and white. Their superior wore a long, gray garment edged with fringe and little white ornaments like fruit, and bound by a gray girdle on which

offerings: a lamb as a burnt offering; a ewe as a sin offering; and a ram as a peace offering—in addition to a basket of unleavened bread, grain offerings and drink offerings, which accompanied the peace offering. They would also shave their head in the outer courtyard of the Jerusalem Temple and then place the hair on the same fire as the peace offering (Numbers 6:18). The Nazarite is described as being "holy unto YHWH" (Numbers 6:8), yet at the same time must bring a sin offering. This has led to divergent approaches to the Nazarite in the Talmud, and later authorities, with some viewing the Nazarite as an ideal, and others viewing him as a sinner. The Nazarites are not to be confused with the *Nazarenes*, who originated as a sect of first-century Judaism. The first use of the term "sect of the Nazarenes" is in the book of Acts, where Paul is accused of being a ringleader of the sect of the Nazarenes. Then, the term simply designated followers of "Yeshua Natzri" (Jesus the Nazarene); but in the first to fourth centuries the term was used for a sect of followers of Jesus who were closer to Judaism than most Christians. They are described by Epiphanius of Salamis and are mentioned later by Jerome and Augustine of Hippo. The name survives into Rabbinic and modern Hebrew as *Notzrim*, a standard Hebrew term for "Christian," and also into the Quran and modern Arabic as *Nasara* (plural of *Nasrani* "Christians"). According to Epiphanius in his *Panarion*, the fourth-century Nazarenes were originally Jewish converts of the apostles who fled Jerusalem because of Jesus's prophecy of its coming siege (during the Great Jewish Revolt in AD 70). In the fourth century, Jerome refers to Nazarenes as those "who accept messiah in such a way that they do not cease to observe the old law." Nazarenes are referenced past the fourth century AD as well. Jacobus de Voragine (1230–1298) described James as a "Nazarene" in *The Golden Legend*. Thomas Aquinas (1225–1274) quotes Augustine of Hippo, who was given an apocryphal book called *Hieremias* by a "Hebrew of the Nazarene Sect." In *Letter 75, Jerome to Augustine*, Jerome writes, "They believe that messiah, the Son of God, was born of the Virgin Mary." Epiphanius of Salamis, in *Panarion* 29.7.2, writes: "They use not only the New Testament but the Old Testament as well, as the Jews do"; and in 29.7.2: "They disagree with Jews because they have come to faith in Christ; but since they are still fettered by the law—circumcision, the sabbath, and the rest—they are not in [full] accord with the Christians."

were inscribed white letters. Around one arm was a band of coarse, gray and white woven fabric as thick as a twisted napkin, one end of which—ornamented with tufted fringe—hung down a little. He wore a collar, or little mantle, almost like that of Archos the Essene, excepting that it was gray and open behind instead of in front. A blank shield was fastened on it in front, while behind it was tied or laced. On the shoulders hung slit lappets. All wore black, shining, puffed caps, with some words stamped on the front; three bands met on top forming a ball, which, like the rim, was white and gray. The Nazarites had long, thick curly hair and beards. I tried to think which of the apostles looked like them, and at last I remembered that it was Paul. His hair and garments, when he persecuted the Christians, were in the style of the Nazarites. I saw him afterward, also, with the Nazarites, for he was one of them. They used to let their hair grow until their vow was accomplished, when they cut it off and burned it in sacrifice. They sacrificed pigeons also. One could assume and fulfill the unfulfilled vows of another. Jesus celebrated the sabbath with them. Jezreel is separated from Nazareth by a mountain range. Not far from it is a well near which Saul once encamped with his army.

In his sabbath teaching the following day, Jesus taught on the baptism of John. He said that, although their piety was praiseworthy, yet excess was dangerous; that there are different ways to salvation; that splits in the community would easily give rise to sects; that, in their pride, they looked down upon their weaker brethren who could not do so much as they themselves, but who should be succored by the stronger. Such teaching as his was very necessary here, for in the outskirts there were people who had mixed with the pagans and who were destitute of rule or direction because the Nazarites had separated from them. Jesus visited these people in their homes and invited them to his instruction on baptism.

Next day Jesus was present at a repast given him by the Nazarites, at which circumcision was spoken of in connection with baptism. For the first time I heard Jesus speaking of circumcision, but I cannot exactly recall his words. He said something to this effect, that the law of circumcision had a reason for its existence, which would soon be taken away, when the people of God would come forth no longer according to the flesh from the family of Abraham, but spiritually from the baptism of the Holy Spirit. Great numbers of the Nazarites became Christians; but they clung so tenaciously to Judaism that many of them, seeking to combine Christianity with it, fell into heresy.

Somewhat over a year later, on Saturday, October 7, AD 30, Jesus taught in the synagogue of Coreae and healed many sick people. This evening, with the close of the sabbath, the feast of Tabernacles also drew to a close. Next morning Jesus preached in the synagogue and, while the Jews took their sabbath promenade, cured many sick who had been brought to a large hall nearby. At the close of the sabbath, while assisting at the entertainment given in the tabernacles, Jesus had a dispute with the Pharisees. The subject under discussion was the prophecies uttered lately by the man born blind (Manahem) and to whom Jesus had given sight. The Pharisees maintained that the same man had already predicted many things that had never come to pass, to which Jesus replied that the Spirit of God had not then descended upon him. During the conversation mention was made of Ezekiel as if his early prophecies relating to Jerusalem had not been fulfilled, to which Jesus responded that the Spirit of God had not come upon him (Ezekiel) until he was in Babylon near the river Chobar, when something was given him to swallow. Jesus's response reduced the Pharisees to silence.

Indeed, Manahem went around the city praising God, singing psalms, and prophesying. The day before he had been to the synagogue, where he was invested with a broad girdle and was admitted by vow among the Nazarites. A priest performed over him the ceremony of consecration. I think he afterward joined the disciples.

Four months later, on the afternoon of Monday, February 12, AD 31, Jesus went with Peter, James, and John to the house of one of the Jewish Elders of the city, a man very well disposed, a friend of Lazarus and Nicodemus, and in secret a follower of Jesus. He had contributed largely to the common fund of the holy women and to the support of the inns. He had two sons and three daughters, all of mature age, he himself being an old man far advanced in years. The children were unmarried. They were Nazarites. All were clothed in white. The old father, whose beard was long and white, was led by the sons to meet Jesus, for he could not walk alone. He was shedding tears of reverential joy. The sons washed the feet of Jesus and the apostles, and presented them with refreshments, fruit and rolls. Jesus was very affable and treated the family with great confidence. He spoke to them of the journeys he was about to make and told them that he would not show himself openly in Jerusalem at the celebration of the coming Passover. He did not remain long in the house, for the people, having found out his whereabouts, had gathered outside and in the forecourt.

Elijah

ELIJAH was a tall, spare man with hollow, reddish cheeks, a bright, piercing glance, a long, thin beard, and a bald head with only a circle of hair around the back. On the top of his head were three large protuberances almost of the form of bulbs, one in the middle, two somewhat toward the forehead. He wore a garment made of two skins fastened together on the shoulder, open at the sides, and bound around the waist with a cord. Over his shoulders and around his knees hung the hair of the beast's skin. He carried a staff in his hand. His shins were far darker than his face.

He was nine months in Abila, and two years and three months in Sarepta with the widow. While at Abila he dwelt in a cave on the eastern slope of the valley not far from the brook. I saw how the bird brought him food. At first there arose a little dark figure like a shadow out of the earth, holding in its hand a thin cake. It was neither man nor beast, it was the evil one come to tempt the prophet. Elijah would not touch the bread, but bade the tempter begone. Then I saw a bird coming to the vicinity of his cave with bread and other food, which it hid under the leaves, as if for itself. It must have been a waterfowl, for it was web-footed. Its head was somewhat broad, by the side of the beak hung bags something like pockets, and under the beak hung a craw. It made a cracking noise with its bill, like a stork. I saw that this bird was

quite at home with Elijah, so much so that on a sign from the prophet it came and went. I saw him pointing to it right and left. I have often seen the same kind of bird with the hermits, also with Zosimus and Mary of Egypt. When Elijah was with the widow of Sarepta, besides the oil and meal that never decreased, other food was sometimes brought him by ravens.

Enoch, Noah's ancestor, opposed that wicked race by his teachings. He wrote much. Enoch was a very good man and one very grateful to God. In many parts of the open fields he raised altars of stone and there the fruits of the earth flourished. He gave thanks to God and offered sacrifice to Him. Chiefly in his family was religion preserved and handed down to Noah. Enoch was taken up to paradise. There he waits at the entrance gate, whence with another (Elijah) he will come again before the Last Day.

Elijah and Symbols of the Mystery of the Immaculate Conception

I SAW the whole earth parched and dried up. I saw Elijah with two servants climbing up Mount Carmel. They first crossed a high ridge, then went up steps cut in the rock to a terrace; from this terrace they ascended by similar steps to a level place from which arose a hill. The hill contained a cave, and up to this Elijah mounted alone. He left his servants on the borders of the level place, that they might look down upon the Sea of Galilee. Its waters were dried up, and its bed lay full of holes, mud, and putrefied carcasses. Elijah sat down, his head resting upon his knees, covered himself with his mantle, and prayed earnestly to God. Seven times did he call to his servants as to whether no cloud out of the sea had yet arisen.

At last I saw in the middle of the sea a white vapor out of which came a little black cloud. In the latter was a small, shining figure

59

which, rising on high, gradually increased in size. As the cloud rose, Elijah perceived in it the figure of a radiant Virgin. Her head was surrounded by rays, her arms were outstretched in the form of a cross, one hand grasping a victor's wreath, and her long garments fell as if bound below her feet. She appeared to be hovering over Palestine. In this vision Elijah learned four mysteries relative to the Blessed Virgin. One was that she would come in the seventh age,[1] and another was the family to which she should belong. He also saw on one shore of the sea a low, spreading tree, and on the other a very lofty one whose summit drooped over upon the lower one.

I saw the cloud break up and fall in fleecy vapors upon certain holy places and upon the abodes of certain pious people who were in prayer. These vapors were bordered by rainbow edges, and in them was the Blessing like a pearl in its shell. I was told that this, though typical, was a true representation of how the preparation for the coming of the Blessed Virgin would develop from those various blessed points.

Soon after this vision Elijah enlarged the cave in which he was accustomed to pray. He made new regulations for the prophet children, of whom from that time some in that cave constantly supplicated for the coming of Mary and honored her advent.

Elijah had by his prayer called up the clouds, and he directed them according to interior enlightenment—otherwise a sudden and destructive rain gust might have resulted from them. At first I saw these clouds dropping down dew, settling in white plains, forming eddies with rainbow-colored edges, and finally dissolving in drops. I recognized some connection between them and the manna in the desert, which in the morning lay brittle and thick like a skin upon the ground. It could be gathered in rolls. I saw the vapors floating along the Jordan. They did not fall in all places indiscriminately, but only here and there—at Salem, for instance,

---

[1] In Brentano's notes the question is posed: "Might this refer to the seven questions of Elijah?"—no doubt in reference to the story of when Elijah, praying on Mount Carmel for rain, six times questioned his servant as to what he saw. The seventh time, the servant replied that he saw a little cloud rising out of the sea. See entry below for Wednesday, March 1, AD 30.

where John baptized at a later period, and at the spot where subsequently his pool of baptism stood. I asked for the signification of the colored edges, and it was explained to me by a certain shell of the sea which, too, has shining colored margins. The shell, when under the sun's rays, absorbs the light, reflects its colors at the edges, thus purifying the ray as it were until in its own center the pure white pearl is formed. I cannot express it, but I understood that that dew and the rain following it did more than what is commonly signified by a refreshing, a watering of the earth. I received the clear assurance that, without this dew, Mary's advent would have been delayed one hundred years longer; while through that watering and blessing of the earth, the different families living on its produce were quickened and enlivened. Thus their flesh received a New Blessing by which it became more purified and ennobled by propagation. The vision of the pearl in its shell bore reference to Jesus and Mary.

The drought that I saw was not confined to the earth alone; there was also a great drought, great sterility, among humankind. But the spray of the fructifying dew descended from generation to generation down to the flesh of Mary. I cannot express it. At times, there appeared upon the colored edges of the cloud one or several pearls, and upon these a human figure, breathing forth something spirit-like which again seemed to amalgamate in the others.

I saw also that, by the great mercy of God, the pious pagans of that age knew that the messiah would be born of a Virgin of Judea. This knowledge was imparted to the star worshippers of Chaldea by the appearance of a vision either in a star or in the heavens. They prophesied concerning it. I saw the same tidings of salvation proclaimed in Egypt.

Elijah was commanded by God to bring together into Judea several pious families scattered to the north, east, and south. He sought for three prophet scholars suited to the mission, and he implored a sign from God by which he might recognize them, for it was a distant and very hazardous undertaking—for those chosen must be most dependable, that they not fail and be slain.

One went north; the second, east; the third, south. This last route led to Egypt, where Israelites could not enter without risk.

I saw the third messenger journeying along the road subsequently traversed by the holy family, and also at Heliopolis. He came at last to a great pagan temple surrounded by numerous buildings and situated in a wide plain. A live bull was worshipped in this temple, and in it were also the image of a bull and other idols. Deformed children were sacrificed to the animal. As the prophet was passing the temple he was seized and led before the priests. Fortunately for him they were exceedingly inquisitive, else perhaps they would have murdered him at once. They questioned him as to whence he came. He answered fearlessly, telling them that a Virgin would be born from whom should proceed the salvation of the world, then would all their idols be shattered. They were amazed and impressed by what they heard and allowed him to go on his way.

But they afterward took counsel together and resolved to make the image of a Virgin. When it was finished they placed it high in the center of the temple roof and in a position as if in the act of floating down. The Virgin's headdress was like that of so many of the other idols, half-woman, half-lion, that were in the temple. The upper part of the arms was close to the body, the forearms extended as if warding off something. Feathers radiated from both upper and lower arms, two clasping together like crests or combs; similar feathers ran down the sides and the middle of the body to the tiny feet. The skirt was without folds. They worshipped this image, and offered sacrifices before it, that it might not shatter to pieces their images of Apis and other idols. But aside from this they remained as they were, sunk in various atrocities, but they now always appealed to this Virgin first. It seemed to me that they had formed her in the image of the various meaningful elements they found in the account of the prophet messenger, and as Elijah had seen her.

It is touching to see how the holy patriarchs, although they had frequent revelations from God, had nevertheless to suffer and to struggle unremittingly in order to keep clear of the abominations that surrounded them. And again, it is affecting to remember in what secret, what painful ways salvation at last came upon earth, while all went well with demonolatry, while all things were made to subserve its interests. When I saw all this: the immense influence exercised by pagan goddesses and the high worship they received over all the earth; and on the other side, when I contemplated Mary's little band, with whose symbolical picture in the cloud of Elijah the philosophers of Cyprus sought to couple their lying abominations; when I saw Jesus, the fulfillment of all promises, poor and patient, standing before them teaching and afterward going to meet his cross—ah, that made me inexpressibly sad! But after all, this is the history of the truth and the light ever shining in the darkness, and the darkness not comprehending it. And so it has been and so it is still, the same old story even down to our own day.

✝ ✝ ✝ ✝ ✝

ON Friday, July 8, AD 29, having continued on his way northward through the night, Jesus and his companions later in the day crossed a spur of the Lebanon foothills and beheld the city of Sidon on the coast of the Mediterranean. Jesus was well received in the city. He had been there once before. In the school he taught of the coming of the messiah and of the downfall of idolatry. Queen Jezebel, who so persecuted Elijah, was from this city. Jesus left his companions in Sidon, and went to a little place more to the south and away from the sea. He wanted to be alone to pray. On one side, this place was entirely flanked by a wood. It had thick walls and was surrounded by vineyards. It was Sarepta, the place in which Elijah was fed by the widow (1 Kings 17:9). The Jews, as also the pagans, had a superstition connected with that fact. They always allowed pious widows to live in the city walls. They thought by so doing they secured themselves from every danger, and could practice every sort of vice in the city. Old men dwelt in the walls at the time of which I am now speaking. Over the following ten days (Saturday, July 9, AD 29, to Tuesday, July 19, AD 29), Jesus lodged with an old man in the city wall, in the house once occupied by that widow who fed Elijah. The old men who then dwelt in the walls were something like hermits. They lived there in accordance with an ancient custom honoring Elijah, meditating and explaining the prophecies, and chiefly engaged in prayer for the coming of the messiah. Jesus taught them concerning the messiah and the baptism of John.

Almost two weeks later, Wednesday, July 20, AD 29, on his return from the shepherds' country to Sarepta, Jesus followed the route trodden by the prophet Elijah when going from the brook Kerith to Sarepta. Jesus taught here and there as he journeyed on, passing by Sidon. On Friday, July 22, and Saturday, July 23, AD 29, Jesus taught and celebrated the sabbath in Sarepta. Then he departed and walked through the night, traveling southward toward Mount Carmel, where the prophet Elijah had once been.

This was the time when John left the desert. He received from on high a revelation concerning the baptism, in consequence of which, shortly before leaving the desert, he dug a well within reach of the inhabited districts. I saw him on the western side of a steep precipice. On his left ran a brook, perhaps one of the sources of the Jordan which rises on Libanus in a cave between two ridges. I saw him as if in ecstasy, and standing by him was a man who drew plans and wrote upon a roll. When John returned to consciousness, he read what had been written, and at once set vigorously to work at the well. The bark roll lay beside him on the ground, weighted by a stone at either end to prevent it from rolling together. John often examined it. It seemed as if all he had to do was there marked down.

Side by side with his vision of the well I beheld a scene in the life of Elijah. I saw him sitting in the desert, sad and dejected, on account of some fault he had committed. At last he fell asleep and had a dream in which it seemed to him that a little boy approached and pushed him with a stick, and that he feared falling into a well nearby. The thrusts he received from the child were so violent as to send him rolling forward some steps. At this stage of the dream an angel awoke him and gave him to drink. This took place on the same spot upon which John now dug the well.

John's second baptism place lay between Jericho and Bethagla, on the western side of the Jordan and opposite Beth-Arabah, which was situated somewhat further down on the east side of the river. It was in this part of the Jordan that Elijah divided the waters with his mantle and passed over with Elisha, who did the same on his return. Elisha also rested here, and over this same spot the children of Israel crossed.

John at this time delivered to his disciples at the Jordan a discourse upon the nearness of the messiah's baptism. He told them that he had never seen him. "But," said he, "I shall as a proof of what I say show unto you the place at which he will receive baptism. Behold, the waters of the Jordan will divide and from their midst an island will arise." At the same moment I beheld the waters of the river dividing, and on a level with its surface appeared a small, white island circular in shape. This happened at the spot over which the children of Israel had crossed the Jordan with the Ark of the Covenant, and at which also Elijah had divided the waters with his mantle.

After the baptism, at the time of the temptation in the wilderness, I saw Jesus at night climbing that steep, wild mountain in the desert now called Mount Quarantania. Three spurs, each containing a grotto, rise one above another. Jesus climbed to the topmost of all, from the back of which one could gaze down into the steep, gloomy abyss below. The whole mountain was full of frightfully dangerous chasms. Four hundred years before, a prophet, whose name I forget, had sojourned in that same cave. Elijah also had dwelt there secretly for a long time and had enlarged it. Sometimes, without anyone's knowing whence he came, he used to go down among the inhabitants of the surrounding district to prophesy and restore peace. One hundred and fifty years ago about twenty-five Essenes dwelt on this mountain. It was at its foot that the camp of the Israelites was pitched when, with the Ark of the Covenant, they marched around Jericho to the sound of trumpets. The fountain whose water Elisha rendered sweet was not far off.

Tempting Jesus, satan seized him fiercely by the shoulders and flew with him over the desert toward Jericho. While standing on the tower I noticed twilight in the western sky. This second flight appeared to me longer than the first. satan was filled with rage and fury. He flew with Jesus, now high, now low, reeling like one who would vent his rage if he could. He bore him to the same mountain, seven hours from Jerusalem, upon which he had commenced his fast. I saw that satan carried Jesus low over an old pine tree on the way. It was a large and still vigorous tree that had stood long ago in the garden of one of the ancient Essenes. Elijah had once lived a short time in its vicinity.

On Wednesday, March 1, AD 30, Jesus delivered in the synagogue of Capernaum an extremely touching discourse upon rain and drought. In it he told of Elijah, who prayed on Mount Carmel for rain and six times questioned his servant as to what he saw. The seventh time, the servant replied that he saw a little cloud rising out of the sea. It became larger and larger until at last it bore rain to the whole country. Then Elijah journeyed through the whole land. Jesus applied those seven questionings of Elijah to the space of time before the fulfillment of the Promise. The cloud he explained as a symbol of the present and the rain as an image of the coming of the messiah, whose teaching should spread everywhere and bear new life to all. Whoever thirsted should now drink, and whoever had prepared his field should now receive rain. This was said so touchingly, so impressively, that all his hearers, as well as Mary and the other holy women, wept.

Four months later, on Monday, July 31, AD 30, Jesus and three of his disciples went to Engannim, where he had some distant relatives who were Essenes. Jesus told them he would cure the sick after the instructions. He taught of the nearness of the kingdom and of the coming of the messiah, citing passages from the scriptures and the prophets and proving that the time had arrived. He mentioned Elijah, his words and his visions, giving the date of the latter, and telling his hearers that the prophet had raised an altar in a grotto to the honor of the Mother of the future messiah. He made a calculation of the time which could be no other than the present, warned them that the scepter had been taken from Judah, and recalled to them the journey of the three kings.

Some weeks later, on the morning of Tuesday, September 19, AD 30, Jesus was conducted by Levites to a home for the blind and the deaf and mute, whom he healed, causing great jubilation in Abila, and afterward taught again from the pillar of Elijah and spoke about the prophet's life. Indeed, I saw on that occasion many things connected with Elijah. Jesus went with the Levites to the cave of Elijah. On the eastern declivity of the valley under a broad, overhanging cliff was a narrow rocky bank upon which Elijah, under shelter of the upper rock, used to sleep on a couch overgrown with moss.

Three days later, on Friday, September 22, AD 30, Jesus taught in the synagogue at Gadara for much of the day. He spoke of Elijah, of Ahab and Jezebel, and of the idol of Baal erected in Samaria. In speaking of Elijah, Jesus said that he had not received bread from ravens, because he had been disobedient.

On the following Tuesday, September 26, AD 30, the feast of Atonement, Jesus taught in the synagogue regarding penance. I saw also during another reading that Elijah, after his death, wrote a letter to King Jehoram. The Jews would not believe it. They explained it in this way: They said that Elisha, who brought the letter to Jehoram, had given it to him as a prophetical letter bequeathed to himself by Elijah. I began myself to think it very strange, when suddenly I was transported to the East and, in my journey, passed the mountain of the prophets, which I saw covered with ice and snow. It was crowned with towers, presenting perhaps the appearance it wore in the time of Jehoram. I went on then eastwardly to paradise, and saw therein the beautiful, wonderful animals walking and gamboling around. There too were the glistening walls and, lying asleep on either side of the gate, Enoch and Elijah. Elijah was in spirit gazing upon all that was then going on in Palestine. An angel laid before him a roll of fine, white parchment and a reed pen. Elijah sat up and wrote, resting the parchment on his knees. I saw a little chariot something like a chair, or throne, coming over an eminence, or around by some steps from the inside of the garden. It was drawn by three marvelously beautiful white animals. I saw Elijah mount it and, as if on a rainbow, journey quickly to Palestine. The chariot stood still over a house of Samaria. I saw Elisha inside praying, his eyes raised to heaven. I saw Elijah letting the letter fall before him, and Elisha bearing the same to King Jehoram. The animals were harnessed to Elijah's chariot, one in front and two behind. They were indescribably lovely, delicately formed animals of the size perhaps of a large roe, snow-white, with long, white, silken hair. Their limbs were very slender, their head always in motion, and on their forehead was an elegant horn bent somewhat toward the front. On the day that Elijah was taken up to heaven I saw his chariot drawn by the same kind of animals.

I saw then also the history of Elisha and the Sunamitess. Elisha performed prodigies even more wonderful than those of Elijah, and in his dress and manners there was something more elegant and refined. Elijah was wholly a man of God with nothing in his manners modeled after other men. He was something like John the Baptist; they were men of the same stamp.

Elijah at the Transfiguration

AT the time of the transfiguration on Mount Tabor, Tuesday, April 3, AD 31, I saw the apostles lying, ravished in ecstasy rather than in sleep, prostrate on their faces. Then I saw three shining figures approaching Jesus in the light. Their coming appeared perfectly natural. It was like that of one who steps from the darkness of night into a place brilliantly illuminated. Two of them appeared in a more definite form, a form more like the corporeal. They addressed Jesus and conversed with him. They were Moses and Elijah. The third apparition spoke no word. It was more ethereal, more spiritual. That was Malachi.[1] I heard Moses and Elijah greet Jesus, and I heard him speaking to them of his passion and of redemption. Their being together appeared perfectly simple and natural. Moses and Elijah did not look aged nor decrepit as when they left the earth. They were on the contrary in the bloom of youth. Moses—taller, graver, and more majestic than Elijah—had on his forehead something like two projecting bumps. He was clothed in a long garment. He looked like a resolute man, like one that could govern with strictness, though at the same time he bore the impress of purity, rectitude, and simplicity. Elijah was quite the opposite of Moses. He appeared to be more refined, more lovable, of a sweeter disposition. But both Elijah and Moses were very dissimilar from the apparition of Malachi, for in the former one could trace something human, something earthly in form and countenance; yes, there was even a family likeness between them. Malachi, however, looked quite different. There was in his appearance something supernatural. He looked like an angel, like the personification of strength and repose. He was more tranquil, more spiritual than the others.

---

[1] See "Malachi" (the essentials of this account are also given in "Moses").

Jesus spoke with them of all the sufferings he had endured up to the present and of all that still awaited him. He related the history of his passion in detail, point by point. Elijah and Moses frequently expressed their emotion and joy. Their words were full of sympathy and consolation, of reverence for the Savior, and of the uninterrupted praises of God. They constantly referred to the types of the mysteries of which Jesus was speaking, and praised God for having from all eternity dealt in mercy toward his people. But Malachi kept silence.

The disciples raised their heads, gazed long upon the glory of Jesus, and beheld Moses, Elijah, and Malachi. When in describing his passion Jesus came to his exaltation on the cross, he extended his arms at the words: "So shall the Son of Man be lifted up!" His face was turned toward the south, he was entirely penetrated with light, and his robe flashed with a bluish white gleam. He, the prophets, and the three apostles—all were raised above the earth.

And now the prophets separated from Jesus, Elijah and Moses vanishing toward the east, Malachi westward into the darkness. Then Peter, ravished with joy, exclaimed: "Master, it is good for us to be here! Let us make here three tabernacles: one for thee, one for Moses, and one for Elijah!" Peter meant that they had need of no other heaven, for where they were was so sweet and blessed. By the tabernacles he meant places of rest and honor, the dwellings of the saints. He said this in the delirium of his joy, in his state of ecstasy, without knowing what he was saying.

✦ ✦ ✦ ✦ ✦

ON Tuesday, May 1, AD 31, Jesus, who had been approached by some pagan philosophers, explained to them the confusion and absurdity of their idolatrous system. He related to them the history of Creation, of Adam and Eve, of the fall, of Cain and Abel, of the children of Noah, the building of the Babylonian tower, the separation of the bad and their gradual falling away into godlessness. He told them that these wicked people, in order to restore their relations with God, from whom they had fallen, had invented all kinds of divinities and had by the evil one been seduced into the grossest error; nevertheless, the Promise that the seed of the woman should crush the serpent's head was inter-

woven with all the poetry, customs, and ceremonies of their nec-
romantic art. It was in consequence of this faint idea they had of
the Promise that so many personages had from time to time
appeared with the vain design of bringing salvation to the world;
but they had given to it instead still greater sins and abominations
drawn from the impure source from which they themselves had
sprung. He told them about the separation of Abraham's family
from the rest of humankind; the education of a special people for
the guarding of the Promise; the guidance, direction, and purification of the children of Israel; and he concluded by telling them
about the prophets, about Elijah and his prophecies, and that the
present time was to be that of their realization. Jesus's words
were so simple, so convincing and impressive, that some of the
philosophers were greatly enlightened, while others, returning to
their mythical accounts, were again entangled in their mazes.

Elijah and the
Mountain of the Prophets

AS *has been told elsewhere in full,*[1] *in the second week of Advent Anne
Catherine was taken by her angel to the highest peak of a mountain in
Tibet, quite inaccessible to man. Here she saw Elijah guarding the treasures of knowledge communicated to men by the angels and prophets
since the Creation. She was told that the mysterious prophetic book in
which she had been allowed to read belonged here. This was not her first
visit. She had often been brought hither by her angel, and also to the ter-
restrial paradise not far distant. These places seemed to be closely connected, as in both she met the same holy custodians:*

As I gazed in wonder I thought, "Why am I here? And why
must I, poor creature, see all this?" And the figure from the tent
spoke: "It is because you have a share in it!" This only surprised
me more, and I descended—or rather I floated down—to where
he sat in the tent. He was clothed like the spirits I am accustomed
to see, his look and bearing like John the Baptist or Elijah. The

---

[1] See "The Mountain of the Prophets," "Paradise," and "Enoch" in *First
Beginnings*. All that can presented here are several specific images from those
two articles relating expressly to Elijah.

books and rolls were very old and precious. On some of them were metallic figures or ornaments in relief; for instance, a man with a book in his hand. The figure told me, or informed me in some way, that these books contained all the holiest things that had ever come from humankind. He examined and compared all, and threw what was false into the fire near the tent. He told me that he was there to guard everything until the time would come to make use of it, which time might have already come, had there not been so many obstacles. I asked if he did not feel tired waiting so long, and he replied "In God there is no time!" He said that I must see everything, and he took me out and showed me around. He said also that humankind did not yet deserve what was kept there.

In the middle of the table lay an immense book that could be opened and shut. It seemed to be fastened to the table, and it was to this the man referred to see if the others were right. I felt there was a door under the table and that a sacred treasure was kept there. The moss-covered seats were placed far enough from the table to allow one to walk around between them and it; behind them lay numbers of books, right and left, the latter destined for the flames. He led me all around them, and I noticed on the covers pictures of men carrying ladders, books, churches, towers, tablets, etc. He told me again that he examined them and burned what was false and useless; humankind was not yet prepared for their contents, another must come first.

I had a deep feeling of the sanctity of the place. I felt that with its waters the salvation of many generations had flowed down into the valleys, that humankind itself had come from this mountain, and had sunk ever lower and lower, and I also felt that heaven's gifts for men were here stored, guarded, purified, and prepared. I had a clear perception of it all; but I could not retain it, and now I have only a general impression.

When I re-entered the tent, the man again addressed me in the same words: "You have a part in all this, you can even take possession of it!" And, as I represented to him my incapacity, he said with calm assurance: "You will soon return to me!" He went not out of the tent while I was there, but moved around the table and the books. The former was not so green as the seats, nor the seats as the things near the towers, for it was not so damp here. The ground in the tent and everything it contained were moss-grown—table, seats, and all. The foot of the table seemed to serve as a chest to hold something sacred. I had an impression that a holy body reposed therein. I thought there was under it a subterranean vault and that a sweet odor was exhaled from it. I felt that the man was not always in the tent. He received me as if he knew me and had waited for my coming. He told me confidently that I should return, and then he showed me the way down.

I know why I went to the mountain. My book lies among the writings on the table and I shall get it again to read the last five leaves. The man who sits at the table will come again in due time. His chariot remains there as a perpetual memorial. He mounted up there in it, and men—to their astonishment—will behold him coming again in the same. Here upon this mountain, the highest in the world, whose summit no one has ever reached, were the sacred treasures and secrets concealed when sin spread among men. The water, the island, the towers, are all to guard these treasures. By the water up there are all things refreshed and renewed. The river flowing from it, whose waters the people venerate, has power to strengthen; therefore is it esteemed more highly than wine. All men, all good things, have come down from above, and all that is to be secured from destruction is there preserved.

The man on the mountain knew me, for I have a share in it. We know each other, we belong together. I cannot express it well, but we are like a seed going through the whole world. Paradise is not far from the mountain. Once before I saw that Elijah lived in a garden near paradise.

I have again seen the prophet mountain. The man in the tent reached to a figure floating over him from heaven leaves and books, and received others in return. He who floated above reminded me very much of St. John. He was more agile, pleasing, and lighter than the man in the tent, who had something sterner, more energetic and unbending about him; the former was to the latter as the New to the Old Testament, so I may call one John, the other Elijah. It seemed as if Elijah presented to John revelations that had been fulfilled, and received new ones from him.

Then I suddenly saw from the white sea a jet of water shoot up like a crystal ray. It branched into innumerable jets and drops like immense cascades and fell down upon different parts of the earth, and I saw men in houses, in huts, in cities all over the world enlightened by it. It began at once to produce fruit in them.

Elisha

WITH certain visions of the Old Testament was connected the instruction I received upon the reason priests no longer relieve or cure, why it is either not in their power, or why it is now effected so differently from what it used to be. I saw this gift of the priesthood possessed by the prophets, and the signification of the form under which it was exercised was shown me. I saw for example the history of Elisha giving his staff to Gehazi to lay upon the dead child of the Sunamitess. In this staff lay spiritually Elisha's mission and power. It was, as it were, his arm—the prolongation of his arm. And here I saw the interior signification and power of a bishop's crozier and a monarch's scepter. If used with faith, they unite both bishop and monarch in a certain way with Him from whom they hold their dignity, with God marking them out at the same time as distinct from all others. But Gehazi's faith was not firm, and the mother thought that only through Elisha himself could help be obtained; and so between Elisha's power from God and his staff, the questionings of human presumption intervened, and the staff cured not. Then I saw Elisha praying and stretching himself, hand to hand, mouth to mouth, breast to breast, upon the boy, and the soul of the boy returned to his body. It was explained to me that this manner of healing referred to, and prefigured, the death of Jesus. In Elisha—by faith and the power conferred by God—were opened again in humankind all the avenues of grace and expiation that had been closed after the fall; that is, the head, the breast, the hands, and the feet. Elisha stretched himself as a living, symbolical cross upon the dead, closed cross of the boy's form, and through his prayer of faith life was restored. He expiated, he atoned for, the sins the parents had committed by their head, heart, hands, and feet—sins that had brought death to their boy.

Side by side with the above I saw pictures of the wounds of Jesus and of his death upon the cross, by which I traced the harmony between Jesus and his prophet Elisha. Since the crucifixion of Jesus, the gift of healing and repairing has existed in full measure among the priests of his Church and in general among faithful Christians; for in the same proportion as we live in him and are crucified with him, are those avenues of grace, his sacred wounds, opened to us. I learned many things of the imposition of hands, the efficacy of a benediction, and the influence exerted by the hand, even at a distance—all was explained by the staff of Elisha, which symbolized the hand. That priests of the present day so seldom cure and bless was shown me in an example significant to that conformity to Jesus upon which depend all such effects.[1]

Now, John the Baptist's second baptism place lay between Jericho and Bethagla on the western side of the Jordan and opposite Beth-Arabah, which was situated somewhat further down on the east side of the river. From this place of baptism to Jericho the distance was about five miles. The direct road led through Bethany and a desert. There was an inn on the route, but built a short distance off from the road. This region was a pleasure resort. The water of the Jordan is beautiful, becoming so clear when allowed to stand. In many places also it is highly odoriferous, owing to the blossoms that fall into it from the bushes in full bloom upon its banks. At times it is very shallow; one can see almost to the bottom, and I saw along the shore deep caves hollowed out of the rocks. It was in this part of the Jordan that Elijah divided the

---

[1] Further elaborating upon this point, Anne Catherine said: "I saw three artists making figures of wax. The first used beautiful white wax, and he was both skillful and intelligent. But he was self-conceited, the image of Christ was not in him, and his work of no value. The second used wax not so white as that of the first, and his indolence and self-will spoiled all. He did nothing at all. The third was awkward and unskillful; but he worked away in his simplicity and with great diligence on common yellow wax. His work was excellent, a speaking likeness, although the features were coarse. I saw renowned preachers vaunting their worldly wisdom, but effecting nothing; while many a poor, unlettered man exercises by the priestly power alone the gift of healing and blessing."

waters with his mantle and passed over with Elisha, who did the same on his return. Elisha also rested here, and over this same spot the children of Israel crossed.

✛ ✛ ✛ ✛ ✛

ON Monday, December 19, AD 29, Jesus departed before daybreak from Thebez. He and his disciples proceeded at first eastward and then, turning to the north, journeyed along the base of the mountain and through the valley of the Jordan toward Tiberias. The passed through Abel-Mehola, a beautiful city, where the mountain extends more to the north. It was the birthplace of Elisha.

On Thursday, February 2, AD 30, Jesus stopped for a while at the house of a rich peasant whose fields covered a whole mountain. On one side the harvest was ripe, whereas on the other they were just about to sow. Jesus taught in a parable of sowing and harvesting (Matthew 13:3, 24). There was here an old, dilapidated teacher's chair formerly used by the prophets. The peasants had restored it very handsomely, and from it Jesus delivered his instructions. Several such places for teaching had been restored since John had here baptized. He had ordered it, for that too was a part of his preparing the way. These teaching chairs had here, as with us, the pictures of the stations, quite gone to ruin since the times of the prophets. Elijah and Elisha had frequented this part of the country.

On Wednesday, February 22, AD 30, in Shunem, a multitude pressed around Jesus that was simply astonishing, and it was ever on the increase. The people surrounded him everywhere, cast themselves down before him, crying and shouting that a new prophet had arisen, one sent by God! Shunem was the native city of the beautiful Abishag who had served David in his old age. Elisha also had had an inn here at which he frequently stopped and in which he had recalled the dead son of his hostess to life. A vision of the same was vouchsafed me, that I might know the place. This city possessed also a free inn for certain travelers. It had been founded as a memorial of Elisha. I know not however whether it was the house that the prophet once occupied, or whether it was another built upon the same site.

On Saturday, July 1, AD 30, Jesus and his disciples arrived at a town where many Jewish exiles lived. He taught on this occasion of Elisha, who with salt had rectified the water near Jericho; then he explained the signification of salt.

On Saturday, August 12, AD 30, when he returned to the synagogue of Nazareth for the close of the sabbath, Jesus found lying in front of it some sick who had been brought there by order of the Pharisees. But he passed through them without curing any. He went on with his discourse in the synagogue, speaking of the plenitude of time, of his own mission, of the last chance of grace, of the depravity of the Pharisees and the punishment in store for them if they did not reform, and impressed upon them the fact of his own coming to help, to heal, and to teach. They became more and more displeased, especially when he said: "But ye say to me, 'Physician, cure thyself! In Capernaum and elsewhere, thou hast wrought miracles. Do the same here in thy native city!' But I say to you no prophet is accepted in his own country." Then comparing the present to a time of famine and the different cities to poor widows, he said: "There was great famine throughout the land in the time of Elijah, and there were many widows in those days, but the prophet was sent to none but the widow of Sarepta. And there were many lepers in the days of Elisha, but he cleansed none but Naaman the Syrian," and so Jesus compared their city to a leper who was not healed.

On Tuesday, September 26, AD 30, I heard a most impressive lesson read in the temple of Dion, for the feast of Atonement, from Jeremiah; and at the same time I saw many scenes in the life of the prophet and much of the horrors of idolatry in Israel. I saw also during another reading in the temple that Elijah, after his death, wrote a letter to King Jehoram. The Jews would not believe it. They explained it in this way: They said that Elisha, who brought the letter to Jehoram, had given it to him as a prophetical letter bequeathed to himself by Elijah.[1] I saw also the history of Elisha and the Sunamitess. Elisha performed prodigies even more wonderful than those of Elijah, and in his dress and manners

---

[1] More on this episode will be found under this date in "Elijah."

there was something more elegant and refined. I saw also how Gehazi, the servant of Elisha, ran after the man whom his master had cured of leprosy (Naaman). It was night and Elisha was asleep. Gehazi overtook Naaman at the Jordan and demanded presents from him in the name of his master. On the next day Gehazi was pursuing his work as if nothing had happened (he was making light wooden screens to be used as partitions between sleeping apartments) when Elisha asked him: "Where hast thou been?" and exposed to him all that had taken place the previous night. The servant was punished with leprosy, which he transmitted to his posterity.

On Wednesday, October 11, AD 30, Jesus journeyed through the valley between Alexandrium and Lebona to Salem. He descended through the forest of Hareth into the plain of Salem. Gardens and beautiful walks lay around the outskirts of the city, which was most delightfully situated. It was not very large, but cleaner and more regular than many others in this region, laid out in the form of a star, the points radiating from a fountain in the center. All the streets ran toward the fountain, and were broken up by beautiful walks. The city at this period, however, had something in its appearance that bespoke decline. The fountain was regarded as sacred. It was once tainted like that near Jericho, but Elisha had, like the one alluded to, purified it by casting into it salt and water in which the holy Mystery had been immersed.

In Michmethath nine days later, on Friday, October 20, AD 30, after confessing their sins to Jesus, a number of people were baptized by Saturnin and Joseph Barsabbas. That evening, as the sabbath began, Jesus taught in the synagogue about the miraculous deeds of the prophet Elisha. The following day, after he had again taught in the synagogue at Aser, his subjects being Abraham and Elisha, Jesus cured many sick, some of them demoniacs and others possessed by the spirit of melancholy. On Friday, October 27, AD 30, I had a vision in which I saw that it was here (Dothan) that the soldiers sent by Jeroboam to seize Elisha were struck blind. Toward noon the following Sunday, Jesus and the disciples returned to the city and to Issachar's, where many people were already assembled. The mistress and domestics were busy preparing the noonday meal. Back of the house was a charming spot in the center of which was a beautiful fountain surrounded by sum-merhouses. The fountain was regarded as sacred, for it had been blessed by Elisha. There were crowds assembled around the foun-tain. Jesus, from the teacher's chair, delivered a discourse to the people on the fulfillment of the Promise, the nearness of the king-dom, on penance and conversion, and of the way to implore the mercy of God and to receive His graces and miracles. He alluded to Elisha, who had formerly taught in this same place. The Syri-ans sent to take him prisoner were struck with blindness. Then Elisha conducted them to Samaria into the hands of their ene-mies, but far from allowing them to be put to death, he enter-tained them hospitably, restored their sight, and sent them back to their king. Jesus applied this to the Son of Man and the persecu-tion he endured from the Pharisees.

On Friday, March 30, AD 31, Jesus was in the synagogue in Ataroth to celebrate the sabbath. The scripture lessons of the day consisted of passages referring to legal impurity contracted by childbirth, to leprosy, to Elisha's multiplication of the bread of the first fruits and the new corn, and to Naaman's cure. The following Friday, in the synagogue in Capernaum, Jesus taught upon the purification of the leprous and the famine of Samaria that ceased so suddenly according to the prophetic words of Elisha.

While in Salamis on Saturday, April 28, AD 31, Jesus went to the waterworks and spoke with the superior about the arrange-ments for the baptismal well, which was not yet under roof and had no means of letting in water. The source of the water was in the mountain range to the west. The new baptismal well had more than four corners, and there were steps leading down into it. A great many Jews and pagans were gathered on the spot, and Jesus told them that next day he would instruct those that wanted to receive baptism. The Jews made frequent allusion to Elijah and Elisha, who likewise had been here.

Tobias
(An Allegory of the Coming of Salvation)

ON *the feast of the Archangel Michael, in September, 1821, Anne Cathe-rine recounted, among other recollections of a vision of the holy angels, the following fragment of the story of Tobias, whom she had seen with the archangel Raphael as his guide:*

I saw many things from the life of Tobias, which is an allegory of the history of the coming of salvation in Israel. It is not merely an imaginative allegory, however, but one that actually happened and was lived. It was shown to me that Sarah, the wife of the young Tobias, was a prototype of Anne the mother of Mary. I will relate as much as I can remember of the many things that happened, but shall not be able to reproduce them in their right order.

The father of Tobias (named Tobias, or Tobit, also) was an emblem of the God-fearing branch of the Jewish race, those who were hoping for the messiah. The swallow, the messenger of spring, indicated the near approach of salvation. The blindness of the elder Tobias signified that he was to beget no more children, and was to devote himself entirely to prayer and meditation; it signified also the faithful, though dim, longing and waiting for the light of salvation and the uncertainty as to whence it was to come. Tobias's quarrelsome wife represented the empty and harassing forms into which the Pharisees had converted the law. The kid she had brought home in lieu of wages had, as Tobias warned her, really been stolen, and had for that reason been handed on to her in return for very little. Tobias knew the people concerned and all about it, but his wife only mocked him. This mockery also indicated the contempt of the Pharisees and formalists for the devout Jews and Essenes and the relationship between the two groups, but I cannot now remember how this was.

The Archangel Raphael was not telling an untruth when he said that he was Azarias, the son of Ananias, for the general meaning of these words is: "The help of the Lord out of the cloud of the Lord."[1] This angel, the companion of young Tobias, represented God's watchfulness over the Blessed Virgin's descent through her

---

[1] This interpretation, alluded to but not definitively established by earlier commentators, is shown by biblical philology to be perfectly correct. CB

The names Azarias and Ananias both occur in Neh. 3:23, where Ananias is in Hebrew *Ananyah*, which may mean "the cloud of the Lord," but the much commoner name is *Hananyah*, "the Lord is merciful." *Azaryah* means "the help of the Lord."

ancestors and His preservation and guidance of the Blessing through the generations that preceded her conception. In the prayer of the elder Tobias, and of Sarah, the daughter of Raguel (I saw both these prayers being brought by the angels at one and the same time before the throne of God and there granted), I recognized the supplications of the God-fearing Israelites and of the daughters of Zion for the coming of salvation, as well as the simultaneous prayers of Joachim and Anna, separated from each other, for the promised offspring.

The blindness of the elder Tobias and his wife's mockery of him also symbolized Joachim's childlessness and the rejection of his sacrifice at the Temple. The seven husbands of Sarah, the daughter of Raguel, who were destroyed by satan, came to their end through sensuality; for Sarah had made a vow to give herself only to a chaste and God-fearing man. These seven men symbolized those whose entry into Jesus's ancestry according to the flesh would have hindered the coming of the Blessed Virgin, and thus the advent of salvation. There was also a reference to certain unblessed periods in the history of salvation, and to the suitors whom Anna had to reject that she might be united to Joachim, the father of Mary.

The maidservant's reviling of Sarah (Tob. 3:7) symbolized the reviling by the pagans and by the godless and unbelieving among the Jews against the expectation of the messiah, for whose coming all God-fearing Jews were, like Sarah, inspired to pray with ever-increasing fervor. It was also an image of the reviling of Anne by her maidservant, whereafter that holy mother prayed with such fervor that her prayer was granted. The fish that was about to swallow young Tobias symbolized the powers of darkness, paganism, and sin striving against the coming of salvation, and also Anna's long barrenness. The killing of the fish, the removal of its heart, liver, and gall, and the burning of this by Tobias and Sarah to make smoke—all these symbolized the victory over the demon of fleshly lusts who had strangled Sarah's seven husbands, as well as the good works and continence of Joachim and Anna, by which they had obtained the blessing of holy fruitfulness. I saw also therein a deep significance relating to the blessed sacrament, but can no longer explain this.

The gall of the fish, which restored the sight of Tobias's father, symbolized the bitterness of the suffering through which the chosen ones among the Jews came to know and share in salvation; it indicated also the entry of the light into the darkness brought about by Jesus's bitter sufferings from his birth onwards.

I received many explanations of this kind, and saw many details of the history of Tobias. I think the descendants of young Tobias were among the ancestors of Joachim and Anne. The elder Tobias had other children who were not godly. Sarah had three daughters and four sons. Her first child was a daughter. The elder Tobias lived to see his grandchildren.

When the Jews returned [to Jerusalem after the Babylonian captivity], Ezra collected all the holy scriptures he could lay his hands on. But of these many were only extracts, lacking portions of the full text. Also, in most cases the original documents had been destroyed. Elkan,[1] the father of Susanna, had copies of many of the proverbs of Solomon as well as many of the psalms. The story of Job, as well as those of Moses, Solomon, and Isaiah, were in the keeping of a scholar whose name I have forgotten, but who was caught together with Sedechias. Solomon's *Song of Songs* is not from the hand of Solomon himself but was composed for him by a prophet. Tobias wrote the first portion of his book, but when he went blind the text was finished by his cousin. His sister's brother then put the book in final order.

✝ ✝ ✝ ✝

AS the birth of Mary approached, I saw three women[2] approaching Anne's abode toward evening. When they arrived they went straight to her apartment back of the fireplace. After a while they all withdrew behind a curtain that concealed an oratory. Anne opened the doors of a little closet built in the wall. In it was a box containing sacred treasures and on either side lights so contrived

---

[1] Most likely Ilkiah, in Sus. 1:2.

[2] Anne's sister Maraha, at Sepphoris; the widow Enue, Elizabeth's sister; and Anne's sister Sobe's daughter [Mary] Salome, wife of Zebedee of Bethsaida, whose later sons and apostles James the Greater and John of Zebedee were not yet born.

that they could be raised in their sockets at pleasure, and resting on upright supports. At the foot of the little altar was a cushioned stool. The box contained some of Sarah's hair, which Anne held in great reverence; some of the bones of Joseph, which Moses had brought with him out of Egypt; something belonging to Tobias, relics of clothing I think; and the little, white, shining, pear-shaped cup from which Abraham drank when he received the Blessing from the angel, and which was later on taken from the Ark of the Covenant and given to Joachim along with the Blessing.

On Sunday, September 25, AD 29, Jesus proceeded to a city named Luz and, going into the synagogue, held a long discourse during which he explained many ancient mysterious symbols from the scriptures. I remember that he spoke of the children of Israel. After crossing the Red Sea they had on account of their sins wandered so long in the desert before being allowed to pass through the Jordan and into the promised land. Now was the actual fulfillment of what was then only typical, for the baptism in the Jordan had been symbolized by the passage of the Israelites through its waters. If they now remained true and observed God's commands, they should indeed be put into possession of the promised land and the City of God. Jesus spoke in a spiritual sense, signifying thereby the heavenly Jerusalem. But his hearers dreamed only of an earthly kingdom and of deliverance from the Romans. Jesus then spoke of the Ark of the Covenant and of the severity of the old law, for whoever approached so near the Ark as to touch it instantly fell dead; but now was the law fulfilled and grace poured forth in the Son of Man. Now, too, was being fulfilled that of which the angels conducting Tobias back into the promised land was a figure; for they who, faithful to the commands of God, had so long pined in captivity, were now to be introduced into the freedom of the law of grace.

On Saturday, January 7, AD 30, Jesus went to join his mother between Capernaum and Bethsaida, the former of which was a little to the north. That evening when the sabbath began Jesus taught in the synagogue of Capernaum. A feast was being celebrated that had some reference to Tobias, who had frequented this part of the country and had done much good. He had also bequeathed property to the schools and synagogues. Jesus gave an instruction on gratitude.

Half a year later, on Sunday, July 16, AD 30, before daybreak of the night between the sabbath and Sunday, Jesus left Adama by the gate through which he had entered, which stood over a bridge. Had they gone by another, they would have had to ferry over the river that ran from Azor to Kedesh, and that near Adama flowed into the Jordan. They left Kedesh to the right and proceeded westward over gently rising mountain terraces. Thisbe was to the left of the little troop on very high ground. Tobias once lived in Thisbe and had there given in marriage his wife's brother, or brother-in-law. He had also been in Amichores, the "city of waters." He might have taken up his abode there permanently were it not that he preferred to go into captivity in order to be useful to his people.

On Thursday, February 8, AD 31, Jesus taught in the synagogue at Naphtali, the birthplace of Tobias. In the evening he arrived at Elkasa. Seven months later, on Friday, September 5, AD 32, at noon, Jesus taught in a house in Kedar. His theme was marriage. Salathiel and his wife were there. Jesus spoke of the conditions for living together in order to become good vine. After the onset of the sabbath Jesus spoke with a man called Nazor, who was responsible for the administration of the synagogue. He was a descendant of Tobias. Jesus then taught about the life of Tobias.

Ezra and the Canon

MANY Jews possessed portions of individual books of the holy scriptures that had been preserved during the time of the Babylonian captivity. Once—as you may know—during the siege, the gate of Jerusalem opened of itself and a number of pious Jews took holy writings to the camp of the Babylonians. The writings were retained and the Jews were sent back into the city. Any writings that remained in the city when it finally fell were burned or otherwise destroyed.

When the Jews returned [to the city after the Babylonian captivity], Ezra collected all the holy scriptures he could lay his hands on. But of these, many were only extracts, lacking portions of the full text. Also, in most cases the original documents had been destroyed. Elkan,[1] the father of Susanna, had copies of many of the proverbs of Solomon as well as many of the psalms. The story of Job, as well as those of Moses, Solomon, and Isaiah, were in the keeping of a scholar whose name I have forgotten, but who was caught together with Sedechias.[2] Solomon's *Song of Songs* is not from the hand of Solomon himself but was composed for him by a prophet. Tobias wrote the first portion of his book, but when he went blind the text was finished by his cousin. His sister's brother then put the book in final order.[3]

All the old holy books were in a state of disorder, and the writings of the prophets were not all collected together. It was Ezra who received from God the command to bring all these things into order. In order to accomplish this he sequestered himself together with seven scribes under tents set up in a field. At the outset several scholars came to this place to speak with Ezra and present him with texts. Later, Ezra was mostly alone with the scribes, often fasting and praying together.

I saw once how in a state of vision an angel gave Ezra a drink like fire, and that thereafter he was able to distinguish in all the writings that which was authentic from that which was not, as also to provide what was sometimes missing in the texts. This latter he did by reading from the scrolls and dictating—under the inspiration of the Holy Spirit—what was lacking to the scribes, who wrote down his words upon scrolls. I beheld also a vision that came to Ezra while he was on a journey.

Anne Catherine believed that Ezra knew of the book (of Ctesiphon),[4] *which was otherwise a secret known only to the prophets. This book still* *exists, she said, for she could see it clearly; indeed, she beheld the whole* *history of this book in great detail, as also its contents, though on*

---

[1] Most likely Ilkiah, in Sus. 1:2.

[2] Presumably Zedekiah, last king of Judah before the destruction of the kingdom by Nebuchadnezzar II, king of Babylon after a siege of Jerusalem in 597 BC. Zedekiah and his followers attempted to escape, making their way out of the city, but were captured on the plains of Jericho.

[3] We repeat here, in the context of Ezra, some material from "Tobias."

[4] See following "The Holy Book of Ctesiphon."

account of all the challenges she faced in her life she could recall only the most salient points—and even those in a somewhat disconnected manner—so that trying to splice together what parts remain may give a rather anomalous impression. And yet all she reported was given quite literally, despite the many gaps.

The Holy Book of Ctesiphon • Zoroaster

I SAW three enlightened pagans to whom much truth was revealed. One of them was a Zoroaster, a Shining Star. Another, with a shorter name, was from one of the nearby countries—India, I think, but am not certain. The third, whose name I have also forgotten, was, I believe, Egyptian.

Some parts of holy scripture were revealed to them. Much of their story is told in the holy book kept in the city of Ctesiphon. They themselves contributed to the book. Later on, Zoroaster extracted many teachings from this book, which he then incorporated into his own religious writings. These men were through God's direction enlightened for the sake of their poor people—but not wholly so, for they remained to some degree in error.

During the Babylonian captivity a multitude of prophets, as well as enlightened pagans, collaborated on the completion of a holy book.

In vision, Anne Catherine beheld this entire process unfold, but was unable to retain the details. All she could say was that the work went on for a long time, that it underwent numerous revisions, and that great sheaves of the writings concerned were destroyed by fire. The book itself, she thought, or a part thereof, had several times been burnt, so that the writing had to be recommenced from the beginning. In general, she said, even as restored, the book was too elevated for humankind. Nevertheless, no more than an extract remains thereof. The primary reason for its failure to survive, Anne Catherine said, was its measureless prolixity.

To continue the work, at one time thirty sages were sequestered under a regimen of prayer and fasting, and they found, when comparing notes, that each was engaged to the same end. This consisted in the separation of the true from the false in old religious books, which was accomplished in connection with revelations and visions regarding them—in a way similar to how I once saw all the authentic passages in the books of Dionysius the Areopagite [whose Latin works stood then on a table nearby] lighting up. This project was worked upon in Chaldea and Egypt. Ezekiel and Jeremiah were at hand in this work. One such contributor, at a certain time, who was engaged in a most efficient, businesslike way with this undertaking, bore the name "little Daniel." He was most adept and skilled at the work and sent on far errands with scrolls and books. Once he was imprisoned, but owing to his work was released—an account of which was also related in the book. It was later said that this Daniel was of the race of Ithamar.[1] There is also some connection with the prophet Daniel.

Once Nebuchadnezzar asked to hear a reading from the book, and had the four Jewish youths[2] called before him. He developed an inclination toward them, granting them so much freedom in the land that the pagan priests said they had won his heart.

Three enlightened pagans (as has been said) contributed revelations to the book also. Among them was one from Bactria who had been with King Cyaxares.[3] His was called Zoroaster. There was another from a region to the East, and another from Egypt. The work of all three was scrutinized, and, having been found in agreement with the whole, added to the book.

There had long been much controversy as to which was the most fitting language for the book, but in the end the most ancient mother tongue of all was chosen, a truly sacred language family of Sanskrit and Zend. The language of the Bactrians and a language of India were their daughters—and both in some ways quite similar in sound to our local, common Plattdeutsch [Low German]. The prophet Malachi had a part in this book also. He was in Babylon at the outset.

Anne Catherine read in the book and could understand many words with pronunciations similar to her native Plattdeutsch. She spoke some-

---

[1] In the Torah, Ithamar is the youngest son of Aaron the high priest. A descendent of Ithamar, Daniel by name, is mentioned among the exiles who returned from Babylon (Ezra 8:2).

[2] Perhaps she means by this Daniel and his friends Shadrach, Meshach, and Abednego (Daniel 3). CB

[3] King of Media, around 600 BC.

what confusedly about the book having been on frequent occasions destroyed and then reconstituted, but could no longer give any order to these things. What follows, however, she was able to report with certainty:

The book covered all the themes which, though contained in sacred scripture, are not always presented clearly, such as: the fall of the angels, the Creation, paradise, the fall into sin, the creatures in paradise, the patriarchs before and after the deluge, many visions and revelations of Adam, Enoch, Seth, Noah, Shem, Abraham, and all the other ancestors; also, much regarding what was revealed to Moses upon the mountain.

The book gave descriptions of all the world ages and patriarchal ages, and refuted the contrived temporal reckonings of deluded peoples. (Anne Catherine saw many such erroneous calculations, and much of the content of the book.) Much also was said of Job therein, as also of the wonderful visions of Joseph and Asenath.

In the book was to be found the unity of the foundations of all religions, and attention was drawn to the truth expressed in the times and events in the books of Moses, from the time of the world's first beginnings up to that of the patriarchs. The names of many individuals were given in the languages of the most varied peoples, for instance that of Noah—for the language from which his name derives is quite other than the Hebrew, which, like the circumcision of Abraham, was given as something new to their ancestor Heber to separate him from the others.[1] Much was said

---

[1] We read elsewhere in the notes: "Heber was not present at the tower of Babylon. God had cast his eye upon Heber in order that, from the pervading evil and confusion of the time, he might be separated off to establish a holy people, and to this end had provided him a new and holy language such as no other people possessed—for in this way might his new people be the better preserved. This language was the Hebrew, or the pure Chaldean tongue. The first mother tongue of all—that spoken by Adam, Shem, and Noah—was a different language, which, however, may still be detected in various dialects. The first true daughter tongues, as has been said, were the Bactrian language, that of the Zend [Commentaries on Zoroastrian texts in an Old Iranian language] and the holy language of the Indians [Sanskrit]. In this pure and holy mother tongue was written the holy book that now lies in Ctesiphon on the Tigris."

in the book also of the mysteries of Egypt, as well as of certain symbols—for example, the ankh and the triangle were often to be met with.

Anne Catherine said also that by means of this book even modern scholars, with all their calculations and admiration for paganism, might be convinced of its truth. She hoped that it would not be forever lost because it had for so long been preserved. She had forgotten for just what destiny the book was intended, but knew it still existed, for she had seen it. At that earlier time the world was not yet ripe to read in it.

Once, shortly before Nebuchadnezzar's madness, the prophets in Babylon lost the book and it came in some way (she no longer retained all the details) into the possession of another people—as it seemed to her, through the agency of a man close to King Cyaxares. Much sorrow was attached to these doings. The man in question had acquired the book through a ruse, or with the help of a king—she was not sure any longer which. She did see, however, how he copied out much from the book onto ox hide, one side of which was still quite raw, and in the process inter-mixed with the text fables drawn from his own religion. This man hailed from either Bactria or Media. She beheld him as though sur-rounded by a star, which she thought was meant to be an indication of his name.[1]

At present the book is kept about sixteen hours northeast of the site of ancient Babylon at a place where two cities are situated close by each other, on opposite sides of the Tigris. The place meant is falling to ruins, as such ancient cities are demolished to make way for the new. The book is secreted in the latter city, whose name has the sound of the disciple whose sight Jesus restored.[2] Many ruins exist there today, and people rather like

---

[1] His name had some reference to "star"—"Zerduscht," "Zerdascht," "Zoro-aster," meaning "shining star." The sound "Stern" was discernible, and the Latin "astrum." She mentioned the name just given—"Zoroaster"—somewhat later, and was of the opinion that the original book incorporated some of his teach-ings. Indeed, that holy book included much drawn from his visionary experi-ences. CB

[2] This would be Ctesiphon: all fits together perfectly. The city Ctesiphon did not yet exist at the time of the Babylonian captivity. At that time the site it later occupied included nothing but a few prisons and towers, and, as it seemed to Anne Catherine, some ovens, perhaps brick kilns. CB

monks still live hidden away here and there among them.[1] But there is a small place there, still inhabited, perhaps the size of Dülmen,[2] with a synagogue. That is where the book is kept.

It lies in a large, beautiful old vault, among many other old books and scrolls, a place where books were brought, or also fetched. The books seemed to some degree jumbled together. The walls of the vault were covered with many old figures, and one such figure, somewhat dark, could be seen above, as though seated upon a wagon. The vault was half buried, its light coming from above. There were other rooms also. The book lay apart from the rest, as though in a forgotten corner. It was fastened to an iron band and lay upon a marble table with ornate legs. It was bound up of large leaves or plates, upon which the writing followed the longer dimension.

Anne Catherine described the page size as at least three to four feet in length, and two to three feet in breadth.

The leaves were of metal, like copper-plate, but flexible, comparable perhaps to horn. But metal it must have been, for the writing was pressed into it, and on the back appeared in relief. In fact, the writing was so deeply graven into the metal that its reverse image sometimes left its mark on the following page. At the top of the outermost plate, or cover, was depicted a great, male figure, a book in his hands and many crowns upon his head.

Anne Catherine had an impression that in our time some travelers had found their way to the book. The people to whom the library belonged she took to be Jews. She saw them dressed in long garments with something like a maniple over the arm. She saw no sign there of a church.

Then she described something, though unclearly, about how the book was opened and viewed, adding that no foreigners were present at that time.

---

[1] Perhaps dervishes, or Jacobites. CB
[2] The town where Anne Catherine was living.

What she meant in saying "It was as though one does something, then does so again," the pilgrim cannot say. Perhaps it was a copy, a duplicate, that had been preserved when the original came into the possession of the Medes?

Anne Catherine was of the opinion that Ezra knew of the book, which otherwise was kept totally secret among the prophets. The book lies there still, for she saw it clear as day. She saw the entire history of the book, and much of its content, quite exactly and in fine detail, though in the press of her life could communicate only the most striking facts about it.

Malachi

WHEN Jeremiah at the time of the Babylonian captivity hid the Ark of the Covenant and other precious objects on Mount Sinai, the Mystery, the Holy Thing, was no longer in it; only its coverings were buried by him with the Ark. He knew, however, what it had contained and how holy it was. He wanted therefore to speak of it publicly, and of the abomination of treating it irreverently. But Malachi restrained him and took charge of the Holy Thing himself. Through him it fell into the keeping of the Essenes,[1] and afterward was placed by a priest in the second Ark of the Covenant.

Malachi was, like Melchizedek, an angel, one sent by God. I saw him not as an ordinary man. Like Melchizedek, he had the appearance of a man, differing from him only inasmuch as was suited to his time. Shortly after Daniel's being led to Babylon I saw Malachi as a boy of seven years, wearing a reddish garment, and wandering around with a staff in his hand. He seemed to have lost his way and took shelter with a pious couple at Sapha of the tribe of Zebulon. They thought him a lost child of one of the captive Israelites and they kept him with them. He was very amiable and so extraordinarily patient and meek that everyone loved him;

---

[1] Anne Catherine was not entirely clear as to whether Malachi himself preserved the Ark and presented it to the Essenes, or whether he transmitted it to the children of the prophets, who in turn later presented it to the Essenes. CB

he could therefore teach and do what he pleased without molestation. He had much contact with Jeremiah, whom he assisted with advice when in the greatest perils. It was through him also that Jeremiah was freed from prison in Jerusalem. The ancient Ark of the Covenant, hidden by Jeremiah on Mount Sinai, was never again discovered. The second Ark was not so beautiful as the first, and it did not contain so many precious things. Aaron's rod was in possession of the Essenes on Horeb, where also a part of the Holy Thing was preserved. The family that Moses appointed as the immediate protectors of the Ark of the Covenant existed till the time of Herod. All will come to light on the Last Day. Then will the mystery become clear, to the terror of all that have made a bad use of it.

Regarding the mysterious book of Ctesiphon, Anne Catherine says, in connection with Malachi:

There had long been much controversy as to which was the most fitting language for the book, but in the end the most ancient mother tongue of all was chosen, a truly sacred language family of Sanskrit and Zend. The language of the Bactrians and a language of India were their daughters—and both in some ways quite similar in sound to our local, common Plattdeutsch [Low German]. The prophet Malachi had a part in this book also. He was in Babylon at the outset.[1]

✝ ✝ ✝ ✝ ✝

ON the evening of Sunday, October 8, AD 30, Jesus and the seven disciples went to the synagogue in Ophra. The Pharisees, speaking with Jesus of Ezekiel, expressed their contempt for the prophet. But Manahem had uttered very profound prophecies of Melchizedek, Malachi, and Jesus. Three days later, on Wednesday, October 11, AD 30, Jesus and the disciples arrived at the town of Salem early in the afternoon. After healing the sick, Jesus taught at the synagogue. During the discourse he spoke of Melchizedek, also of Malachi, who had once sojourned here and who had prophesied the sacrifice according to the Order of Melchizedek.

---

[1] See "The Holy Book of Ctesiphon."

Jesus told them that the time for that sacrifice was drawing near, and that those ancient prophets would have been happy to have seen and heard what they now saw and heard.

Three weeks later, on Tuesday, October 31, AD 30, Jesus began the morning talking with his elderly relatives, then traveled with his disciples to Abez. Here, after teaching at the well (Saul's well) east of the town, Jesus blessed a number of children and then taught in the synagogue. The brook flowing through this valley was called Kadumin. It is mentioned in Deborah's *Canticle*. The prophet Malachi once sojourned here for a time and prophesied. Abez was about three hours from the pagan city Scythopolis. The following Friday, November 3, AD 30, Jesus taught in the synagogue at Dabrath, near Tabor. On the southeastern side of Tabor lay a cave with a little garden in front. There the prophet Malachi had often sojourned. Farther up the mountain were another cave and garden where Elijah and his disciples sometimes lived retired, as upon Carmel. These caves were now held as shrines by pious Jews, and thither they used to go to pray.

The following day, Saturday, November 4, AD 30, before Jesus returned to the synagogue for the closing services of the sabbath, the Herodians sent messengers to request him to meet them at a certain place in the city, since they wanted to speak with him. Jesus replied to the messengers with a severe expression: "Say to those hypocrites that they may open their double-tongued mouths against me in the synagogue, for there shall I answer them and others." He added other hard names, and then went to the school. The sabbath reading again treated of Jacob and Esau, of grace and the law, and of the children and servants of the Father. Jesus inveighed so vehemently against the Pharisees, the Sadducees, and the Herodians that their fury increased at each moment. The necessity in which Isaac had been of removing from place to place and the filling up of the wells by the Philistines, Jesus applied to his own teaching mission and the persecution he endured from the Pharisees. Passing then to Malachi, he announced the fulfillment of his prophecy: "My name shall be magnified upon the border of Israel. From the rising of the sun even to the going down, my name is great among the Gentiles." Then he made known to them all the ways he had traversed on either side of the Jordan in order to glorify the name of the Lord. He declared that he would continue his course to the end, and in severe language he quoted against them these other words of the prophet: "The son shall honor the father, and the servant his master." His enemies were confounded and had nothing to reply.

Four days later, on Wednesday, November 8, AD 30, Jesus gave one of the most powerful discourses he had yet delivered. He prayed before he began and then told his hearers that they should not be scandalized at him if he called God his Father, for whosoever does the will of the Father in heaven, he is His son; and that he really accomplished the Father's will, he clearly proved. Hereupon he prayed aloud to his Father and then commenced his austere preaching of penance after the manner of the ancient prophets. All that had happened from the time of the First Promise, all the figures and all the menaces, he introduced into his discourse and showed how, in the present and in the near future, they would be accomplished. He proved the coming of the messiah from the fulfillment of the prophecies. He spoke of John, the precursor and preparer of the ways, who had honestly fulfilled his mission, but whose hearers had remained obdurate. Then he enumerated their vices, their hypocrisy, their idolatry of sinful flesh; painted in strong colors the Pharisees, Sadducees, and Herodians; and spoke with great warmth of the anger of God and the approaching judgment, of the destruction of Jerusalem and the Temple, and of the diverse woes that hung over their country. He quoted many passages from the prophet Malachi, explaining and applying them to the precursor, to the messiah, to the pure oblation of bread and wine of the new law (which I plainly understood to signify the holy sacrifice of the mass), to the judgment awaiting the godless, to the second coming of the messiah on the Last Day, and spoke of the confidence and consolation those that feared God would then experience. He added moreover that the grace taken from them would be given to the pagans.

As the sabbath began the following Friday, November 24, AD 30, the Pharisees were still together. They ran through all kinds of ancient writings relative to the prophets, their manner of life, their teachings, and their actions. They dwelt especially upon Malachi, of whom many traditions were still extant, and compared what they found with the doctrine of Jesus. They were obliged to give Jesus the preference and admire his gifts, though they continued to criticize his teachings.

Some three weeks later, on Thursday, December 14, AD 30, from Bethanat, Jesus went with the apostles and disciples northward around Saphet to Galgala, a large, beautiful place through which ran a great highway. He went with his followers to the synagogue. There were some Pharisees in this city. Jesus preached vehemently against them, explained all the passages of the prophet Malachi that spoke of the messiah, the precursor John, and of the new, clean sacrifice. He ended by announcing that the time for the fulfillment of these prophecies had arrived.

Around ten o'clock the following Wednesday, December 20, AD 30, Jesus went into Abram, and in the synagogue taught of the beatitudes and from some passages of the prophet Malachi.

On Thursday, February 1, AD 31, Jesus continued his teaching on the bread of life on the road leading into Bethsaida, this time saying quite plainly that he was the bread of life (John 6:35–51). All these instructions were accompanied by full explanations and quotations from the *Law* and the *Prophets*. But most of the Jews would not comprehend them. They took all literally according to the common, human acceptation, and again asked: "What mean these words, that we should eat him, and have eternal life? Who, then, has eternal life, and who can eat of him? Enoch and Elijah have been taken away from the earth, and they say that they are not dead; nor does anyone know whither Malachi has gone, for no one knows of his death. But apart from these, all other men must die." Jesus replied by asking them whether they knew where Enoch and Elijah were and where Malachi was. As for himself, this knowledge was not concealed from him. But did they know what Enoch believed, what Elijah and Malachi prophesied? And he explained several of their prophecies. Jesus resumed and continued his instructions on the bread of life the following day, Friday, February 2, AD 31. He said, "The bread that I will give is my flesh for the life of the world." At these words, murmurs and whispers ran through the crowd: "How can he give us his flesh to eat?" Jesus continued and taught at length as the gospel records (John 6:52–59). He then explained many passages from the prophets, especially from Malachi, and showed their accomplishment in John the Baptist, of whom he spoke at length.

Malachi at the
Time of the Transfiguration[1]

ONCE atop the mountain, Jesus summoned his companions to pray on their knees with upraised hands. They knelt in a half-circle around him. He knelt also, while leaning against a projecting rock, and spoke—praying and teaching them the Lord's Prayer, interspersing the several petitions with verses from the Psalms and with instructions, wonderfully profound and sweet, upon the mysteries of Creation and Redemption. In the beginning of his instruction Jesus told them he would show them who he is, that they would behold him glorified, so they might not waver in faith when his enemies mocked and maltreated him—when they would behold him in death, shorn of all glory.

Later, the apostles lay in ecstasy rather than in sleep, prostrate on their faces. Then I saw three shining figures approaching Jesus in the light. Their coming appeared perfectly natural. It was like that of one who steps from the darkness of night into a place brilliantly illuminated. Two of them appeared in a more definite form, a form more like the corporeal. They addressed Jesus and conversed with him. They were Moses and Elijah. The third apparition spoke no word; it was more ethereal, more spiritual. That was Malachi.

I heard Moses and Elijah greet Jesus, and I heard him speaking to them of his passion and of redemption. Their being together appeared perfectly simple and natural. Moses and Elijah did not look aged or decrepit, as when they left the earth. They were on the contrary in the bloom of youth. But both Elijah and Moses were very dissimilar from the apparition of Malachi, for in the former one could trace something human, something earthly in form and countenance; yes, there was even a family likeness between them. But Malachi looked quite different. There was in

---

[1] Wednesday, April 4, AD 31. See related accounts in "Moses" and "Elijah."

his appearance something supernatural. He looked like an angel, like the personification of strength and repose. He was more tranquil, more spiritual than the others. Jesus spoke with them of all the sufferings he had endured up to the present and of all that still awaited him. He related the history of his passion point by point. Elijah and Moses frequently expressed their emotion and joy. They constantly referred to the types of the mysteries of which Jesus was speaking, and praised God for having from all eternity dealt in mercy toward his people. But Malachi kept silence.

The disciples raised their heads, gazed long upon the glory of Jesus, and beheld Moses, Elijah, and Malachi. When in describing his passion Jesus came to his exaltation on the cross, he extended his arms at the words "So shall the Son of Man be lifted up!" His face was turned toward the south, he was entirely penetrated with light, and his robe flashed with a bluish white gleam. He, the prophets, and the three apostles—all were raised above the earth. And then the prophets separated from Jesus, Elijah and Moses vanishing toward the east, Malachi westward into the darkness.

✢ ✢ ✢ ✢ ✢

ABOUT three weeks later, on Tuesday, April 24, AD 31, just before setting sail for Cyprus, Jesus and a few disciples crossed the Leontes river and came to an inn. That evening the Jews tendered Jesus at the inn a festive entertainment, at which they took the opportunity to express to him in a body their sincere gratitude for his not having despised them, for his coming to them, the lost sheep of Israel, and proclaiming to them salvation. They had kept their genealogical table in good order. They now laid it before Jesus and were deeply moved at finding that they had sprung from the same tribe as himself. It was a joyful entertainment, and at it all assisted. They spoke much of the prophets, especially of Elijah, whom they named with words of great affection, recounting his prophecies of the messiah, also those of Malachi, and saying that the time for their fulfillment must now be near. Jesus explained everything to them and promised to introduce them into the land of Judea.

Two weeks later, on Monday, May 7, AD 31, while in a small place near Kythria in Cyprus, Jesus spoke with some Rechabites,[1] who entertained a great veneration for Malachi. They told Jesus that they esteemed him an angel of God, that he had come as a child to certain pious people, that he had frequently disappeared for a time, and that no one knew whether he was now really dead or not. They dwelt at length on his prophecies of the messiah and his new sacrifice, which Jesus explained as relating to the present and the near future.

That Friday, May 11, AD 31, Jesus and the disciples took a walk with seven (formerly pagan) philosophers who had received baptism. The latter asked him about the Persian king Jamshid, who had received a golden blade from God with which he had divided many lands and shed blessings everywhere. Jesus's words upon Jamshid and Melchizedek were so clear, so indisputable, that the philosophers exclaimed in astonishment: "Master, how wise you are! It would almost seem as if you lived in that time, as if you knew all these people even better than they knew themselves!" Jesus said to them many more things concerning the prophets, both the greater and the minor, and he dwelt especially upon Malachi. On the morning of the following Wednesday, May 16, AD 31, Jesus gave an instruction at his inn to the baptized pagans and aged Jews. He took for his subjects the feast of Pentecost, the law given upon Sinai, and baptism, all of which he treated in deeply significant terms. He touched upon many passages relating to them in the prophets. He spoke also of the holy bread blessed at Pentecost, of Melchizedek's sacrifice, and of that foretold by Malachi. He said that the time for the institution of that sacrifice was drawing near, that when this feast would again come round, a new grace would have been added to baptism, and that all the baptized who would then believe in the consoler of Israel, would share in that grace.

On Friday, July 6, AD 31, Jesus went from Salcha with his followers for about an hour and a half along the so-called Way of David, which, following the windings of the valley, led down to the Jordan. This road was deep, a kind of hollow, in which water

---

[1] See below, "The Rechabites."

sometimes flowed. When journeying through this country Abraham saw a supernatural light on this road and had a vision; and when David, upon the advice of Jonathan, sought safety for his parents in the region of Mizpah, he lay concealed here with three hundred men, from which circumstance it received the name David's Way. David here received from God a prophetic vision in which he saw the caravan of the three kings and heard, as if from the heavens open above him, melodious chanting proclaiming the praises of the promised consoler of Israel. Malachi also, being obliged to flee after a battle, followed a mysterious light that led him to this region where he too lay hid for a time; and the three holy kings, giving rein to their camels upon leaving the confines of Salcha and entering this road, descended by it singing sweet hymns of thanksgiving.

Malachi in
Connection with the Passion

THE Last Passover supper was held on Thursday, April 2, AD 33 in the larger building (of the cenacle), that is, the principal one, which contained the dining hall rented by Heli. It was in this house, in the time of King David, that his valiant heroes and generals exercised themselves in arms; here too, before the building of the Temple, had the Ark of the Covenant been deposited for a long time. Traces of its presence were still to be found in an underground apartment. I have seen also the prophet Malachi hidden in this vault. There it was that he wrote his prophecies of the most blessed sacrament and the sacrifice of the new law.

Later that evening Jesus stood before Annas and Caiaphas, staggering from side to side. With freezing irony, Annas addressed him: "Who are you? What kind of a king are you? What kind of an Envoy are you? I think you are only an obscure carpenter's son. Or are you Elijah, who was taken up to heaven in a fiery chariot? They say that he is still living. You too can render yourself invisible, for you have often disappeared. Or perhaps you are Malachi? You have always vaunted yourself upon this prophet and did love to apply his words to yourself. It is also reported of him that he had no father, that he was an angel, and that he is not yet dead.

What a fine opportunity for an imposter to give himself out for him! Say, what kind of a king are you? You are greater than Solomon! That too is one of your speeches. Come on! I shall not longer withhold from you the title of your kingdom!"

Vision Journey with Malachi

I HAD a most difficult night, during which I undertook an arduous journey, for I had to discharge a mission. A thousand obstacles stood in my way: I was pursued, robbers seized upon me, I suffered thirst and hunger, heat, exhaustion, and was chased by evil spirits. But in spite of all I fulfilled my commission, which was to take on the form of Malachi of Jogbeha,[1] who had acted as a spy or scout for Moses,[2] and travel under this guise to a certain man who dwelt upon an African island in order to convey to him a message. And since this Malachi had resided in Jogbeha, I had to clothe myself as he would have done.

There was something amusing about this, however—as though I were myself descended from this same Malachi. But another spirit accompanied me, the prophet Malachi, who instructed me throughout. And so I journeyed—in great danger and need— through the land of Judea, the wilderness of Sinai, and along Arabia by the Red Sea, which I then crossed over. Along the way I saw everything that had formerly happened there that bore some reference to my mission. I saw also many circumstances in the life of the prophet Malachi himself, and those of other prophets from the time of the Babylonian captivity, as well as something of Ezra, holy scripture, and another holy book.[3]

I came in due course to an island upon which were five places whose inhabitants seemed to vacillate between Judaism and the religion of the Turks.[4] I had to go to an elderly priest charged with settling some sort of religious dispute—the point at issue having

---

[1] Identified with a town near Amman, capital of Jordan.
[2] See "Malachi, Spy of Moses," where portions of this vision are recounted.
[3] See "Ezra and the Canon" and "The Holy Book of Ctesiphon • Zoroaster."
[4] The Muslim religion.

to do with the Old Testament and the laws of Moses, to which this priest was much attached.

And so I had to explain to him some prophecies—for instance the words "Thou art a priest forever after the order of Melchizedek."[1] I asked him if Aaron had been such a priest; if Moses on Sinai had received other than an outward, disciplinary law for a people who had believed in an anterior sacrifice of bread and wine; if this sacrifice was not holier and, properly speaking, the beginning and the end; if Abraham had not offered to Melchizedek bread and wine, paid him tithes,[2] and bowed down before the sacrifice of his Church. I cited texts from the Psalms, such as "The Lord said to my Lord," etc., and passages from Malachi upon the unbloody sacrifice. I exhorted him to go to Rome, there to be instructed and to have the above passages particularly explained.

After these words I saw him rise, take a bible, and consult the texts quoted. These people have no fixed abodes, but they seemed about the work of forming some, for they took possession of land, enclosed it with walls, and built mud huts. There were, roundabout, several such settlements, and no city dwellers among them.

The people are not entirely Jewish, but followed some tenets of Christianity. They entertained a hatred for certain particularly strict Christians,[3] with whom they would not break bread. It seems to me they were circumcised and eager to receive instruction. It was for this reason that the man should travel to Rome and receive training there. I had also to tell him, as I have already said, that while there he should request that such points as I had just related to him be emphasized in the instruction offered.[4]

This journey was made as if it happened in the present, for in many places the desert was far greener than when Mary passed by on the Flight into Egypt. Nevertheless, at particular places I had

---

[1] Psalm 110:4, Heb 5:6–10; 6:20; 7:1–21; 8:1.

[2] See Gen 14:18–20.

[3] Did she mean Greeks, Armenians, Maronites, or others? CB

[4] Then Anne Catherine spoke much of something rather uncertain, for it now escaped her mind—it was a complicated subject, to do with twelve bishops. CB

visions from olden times. For instance I passed Gaza on my right, where Samson carried away the gate and died, all of which I saw in pictures.[1] Then I traveled more to the east, whereas the Mother of God had journeyed to the south.

I passed through regions inhabited by multitudes of people, toward the Red Sea, and into the land were Job passed his final years. I encountered all sorts of caravans led by wild riders and passed by the site where Seth's grave is believed to be. I saw also Midian, where Jethro had lived, in which region two of Esau's sons by his first wife married among the people of Midian.

As has been said, as I saw these things—accompanied and instructed by the prophet Malachi—I was clothed in the garments of that servant of Jethro, Malachi of Jogbeha, and felt myself to be a descendent of this man.[2]

It has happened before that the spirit of one prophet comes to work in that of another.[3] It seems to me that those prophets belong to the line of the Midianites. Good deeds of the patriarchs benefit the children coming after them. The remaining merit of the patriarchs animates still the best among their descendents.[4] Those who engage in evil works break these threads, obstruct the line of transmission,[5] whereas those who do good works combat evil within themselves and clear it away, so that, after the Blessing, the springs of old may flow again, extending the source of benediction.[6]

I can no longer say whether the many toilsome difficulties I encountered during the course of this journey came from people

---

[1] See "Samson and Delilah."

[2] Or did Anne Catherine perhaps mean by this a prophetic relationship? Several years prior to this she said in her sleep: "We are as seeds strewn throughout the world, and are known to one another." CB

[3] In this case, in the spirit of Anne Catherine.

[4] It seems that through her love and joy in the deeds of Malachi of Jogbeha—to whom [she felt] she was related—Anne Catherine took up the threads representing the legacy of his deeds and brought them to bear on his progeny. So at least it seems to me, from her explanations in similar instances. CB

[5] Anne Catherine says, literally, "block the channel."

[6] Here Brentano notes that he is putting into his own words what Anne Catherine had to say on this subject.

now living in the places I visited, or from spirits. Perhaps they originated from those people's spirits, as working through them. For the realm of the spirits is grander, richer, and more orderly than is the realm of humankind, and there are among the spirits some engaged in constant activity against all who turn to God's kingdom in prayer, beseeching it to come down according to the command of Christ.

Later on, calling these things again to mind, Anne Catherine repeated that the inhabitants of the island of which she had been speaking were Christians of a sort, adding that in the early days an apostle must have come to them, for many traces of Christianity were still to be found. They still greatly yearned for their teacher, whose name, however, they had forgotten. They had over time come to congregate on one side of the island, which was larger than Cyprus. Anne Catherine believed that in the vicinity Protestant missionaries were to be found, some of whom had made their way among them—and it was this that had led to considerable curiosity among the islanders, as well as deliberations regarding the religion [of the Protestants] and some dissension as to what position they should adopt in this regard. She felt also that in the neighboring district was a Catholic missionary who had, however, not been able to reach them.

Later, while reading up on this subject, the pilgrim found out that the description of the region, as also the traces of Christianity still to be found among its people, matched up with the cross-bearing pagans of the Arabian island of Socotora[1]—as did also the aversion they harbored toward certain forms of Christianity, just as Anne Catherine had said.

The pilgrim then asked Anne Catherine whether the island she had described was named Socotora, to which she answered in the affirmative, and then added the following:

The apostle Thomas was the first to come among the people of this island.[2] And the teacher for whom they still so yearned was

---

[1] Socotora (Socotra or Soqotra) is an island and an archipelago of four smaller islands in the Arabian Sea. The territory is now part of Yemen.

[2] See "Thomas" in *People of the New Testament II* for more on the island of Socotora.

Pantaenus of Alexandria,[1] who had taught their ancestors. Francis Xavier visited this island also. The inhabitants held strict fasts, but prayed to the moon, and clung with astonishing tenacity to the cross, without, however, knowing why they did so. Their priests carried it always upon their person (it was quite large) and affixed it to their staffs. The people were circumcised and practiced poly-gamy. They had a book wherein a great deal was said of Job and Abraham, though with truths and untruths jumbled together. Recently, however, they had found a book in which much was said of Noah—although under another name—and also about the tower of Babel, Nimrod, and the fathers [of ancient peoples]. (Anne Catherine did not know whether or not these accounts were drawn from the Old Testament.)

The Rechabites

IN Ephron there were Levites who belonged to an ancient sect called Rechabites. On Wednesday, September 13, AD 30, Jesus reproached them for the severity of their interpretation of the law, and advised the people not to observe many of their prescriptions. In his instruction he alluded to the punishment of those Levites of Bethsames who had irreverently (too curiously) gazed upon the Ark of the Covenant, which had been brought back by the Philistines. The Rechabites were descended from Jethro, the father-in-law of Moses. In early times they lived under tents, carried on no husbandry, and abstained from the use of wine. They exercised the office of chanters and gatekeepers in the Temple. Those men

---

[1] Pantaenus [Brentano has the spelling Panthanus in his notes] was a Stoic philosopher teaching in Alexandria who converted to the Christian faith and sought to reconcile his new faith with Greek philosophy. His most famous student—Clement of Alexandria—was his successor as head of the Catechetical School. Although no writings by Pantaenus are extant, his legacy is known by the influence of the Catechetical School on the development of Christian theology, in particular in the early debates on the interpretation of the bible, the Trinity, and christology. In addition to his work as a teacher, Eusebius of Caesarea reports that Pantaenus was for a time a missionary, traveling as far as India, where—according to Eusebius—he found Christian communities using the Gospel of Matthew, supposedly left them by the apostle Thomas.

who near Bethsames had, contrary to orders, gazed upon the returning Ark, and had for so doing been punished with death, were Rechabites who there dwelt under tents. Jeremiah tried once, but in vain, to make them drink wine in the Temple. He afterward held up to Israel as an example the obedience of these men to their laws. In Jesus's time they no longer dwelt under tents, though they still preserved many of their peculiar customs. They wore a hairy ephod (a scapular) as a cilicium[1] next to their skin, and over that a garment made from the skins of beasts. Their outer robe was white, beautiful and clean, and was confined by a broad girdle. One of the points in which they differed from the Essenes was in their better mode of dressing. Their rules relating to purity were excessively strict, and they had very singular customs with regard to marriage. They passed judgment after examining blood drawn from the candidate for marriage. According to this test they decided whether he should marry or not, enjoining it upon some of their sect and forbidding it to others. In early times they were to be found in Argob, Jabesh, and in Judea. They offered no opposition to the words of Jesus, but took his instructions and his reproaches alike humbly and in good part. He reprehended them most of all for their unmerciful severity to adulterers and murderers, to whom they granted no quarter.

The following day, September 14, AD 30, after healing the sick of Ephron, Jesus went with his disciples and several of the Rechabites about five hours to the north to Betharamphtha-Julias, a beautiful city situated on a height. On the way he gave an instruction near a mine from which was obtained the copper that was wrought in Ephron. There were some Rechabites in Betharamphtha, and among them priests. Those of Ephron appeared to me to be under their jurisdiction.

That Saturday, September 16, AD 30, Jesus taught in the synagogue in the morning and then cured many sick people. Abigail,[2] who was held in esteem by the inhabitants of Betharamphtha,

---

[1] Hair shirt.

[2] See "Abigail, Repudiated Wife of Philip the Tetrarch" in *People of the New Testament V.*

sent gifts down from her castle to the Jews for the more honorable entertainment of Jesus and his disciples. On the first of the month of Tisri the New Year was celebrated, which fact was announced from the roof of the synagogue by all kinds of musical instruments, among them harps and a number of large trumpets with several mouthpieces.

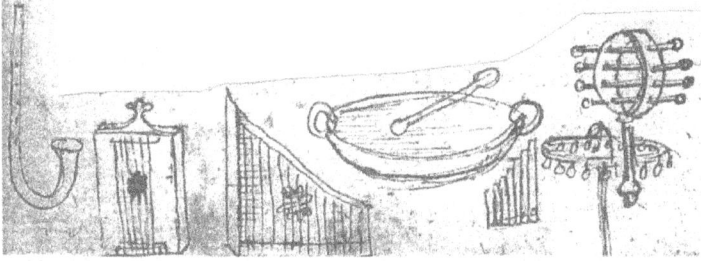

The different classes of people had different customs. During the night, many persons—most of them women clothed in long garments and holding lighted lanterns—prayed upon the tombs. I saw too that all the inhabitants bathed, the women in their houses and the men at the public baths. As bathing was very frequent among the Jews, and water not abundant, they made use of it sparingly. They performed their ablutions today at the baths outside the city, in water perfectly cold. Mutual gifts were interchanged, the poor being largely remembered. They commenced by giving them a good entertainment, and on a long rampart were deposited numerous gifts for them, consisting of food, raiment, and covers. Every one that received presents from his friends bestowed a part of them upon the poor. The Rechabites present superintended and directed all things. They saw what each one gave to the poor and how it was distributed. They kept three lists, in which they secretly recorded the generosity of the donors. One of these lists was called the book of life; another, the middle way; and the third, the book of death. It was customary for the Rechabites to exercise all such offices, while in the Temple they were gatekeepers, treasurers, and above all chanters. This last office they fulfilled on today's feast.

On the morning of Monday, September 18, AD 30, after healing many people, Jesus spoke in the synagogue. He taught about

Isaac's sacrifice (Genesis 22), which was associated with the two-day New Year festival at the start of the month of Tishri.

Then, with the disciples and accompanied by the Levites, Jesus went three hours to the northwest toward a deep dale through which the brook Kerith flowed to the Hieromax. In this dale lay the beautiful city of Abila, built around the source of the brook Kerith. The Levites accompanied him to a mountain that stood halfway on the road, and then went back to Betharamphtha. It was three o'clock in the afternoon when the Levites of Abila, among whom were several Rechabites, received Jesus outside the city. Three of the disciples from Galilee were with the Levites awaiting his arrival. They conducted him at once into the city and to a very lovely fountain, the source of the brook Kerith.

On the morning of Wednesday, September 20, AD 30, after Jesus had again taught and cured the sick in the synagogue, he went with the disciples, the Levites, the Rechabites, and some of the citizens, to the western heights of the mountain. There making a circuit of about an hour, he went through the vineyards giving instructions. On this mountain range, as far as Gadara, were numerous rocky projections like mounds. Some had been raised by nature, others formed by the hand of man, and around them vines were planted, the vinestocks as thick as one's arm. They were planted far apart and threw out their branches to a great distance. The bunches of fruit were often as long as one's arm, while the single grapes were large as plums. The leaves were larger than those of our vines, though small when compared with the fruit. The Levites put many questions to Jesus upon different portions of the Psalms that treated of the messiah. They said: "Thou art certainly the greatest prophet after the messiah! Thou canst explain these points to us." Among other things there was question of the words: *"Dixit Dominus Domino meo,"*[1] and of him that with blood-besprinkled garments trod the wine press alone. Jesus explained all to them with its profound signification and applied it to himself. During this little instruction they sat around one of the vine hills eating grapes. The Rechabites, however, would not touch the fruit, because they were forbidden to drink wine. But

---

[1] "The Lord said unto my Lord," Psalm 110:1.

Jesus challenged them upon their abstinence and commanded them to eat, saying that if they sinned by so doing, he would take the guilt upon himself. When they brought forward their law as an excuse for not complying, I heard them saying that Jeremiah, on the command of God, had once forbidden it and they had obeyed. But now that Jesus ordered otherwise, they hearkened to his word. Toward evening they returned to the city and assisted at another entertainment, to which the poor were admitted. Then Jesus taught in the synagogue and afterward went to the house of the Levites, where he passed the night on the roof under a tent.

About seven months later, on the morning of Friday, May 4, AD 31, Jesus visited an iron mine near Kythria (on Cyprus). He addressed the workers and spoke the words recorded in Luke 6:31. He then entered the town and was greeted by the Jewish Elders and also by two of the philosophers from Salamis. Jesus went next to the house of the elder of the synagogue, where several of the literati were assembled, among them some belonging to the sect of Rechabites. These last named wore a garb somewhat different from the other Jews, and their manners and customs were peculiarly rigorous. Of these, however, they had already laid aside many. They had a whole street to themselves and were especially engaged in mining. They belonged to that race that settled in Ephron, in the kingdom of Basan, in whose neighborhood also mining was carried on.

Two days later, Sunday, May 6, AD 31, there appeared to be either a feast or a fast among the Jews, for there was morning service in the synagogue, that is, prayer and preaching. That over, Jesus left the city by the north side with all his disciples and some pagan youths. His little band was joined by some Jewish doctors and several Rechabites, so that there were altogether fully one hundred men. They pursued their journey for about an hour to a place that was the principal seat of the bee-raising industry. Far off toward the rising sun stood long rows of white beehives, about the height of a man, and woven, I think, of rushes or bark. They had many openings and were placed one above another. Every group had in front of it a flowery field, and I noticed that balm grew here in abundance. Each field, or garden, was hedged in, and the whole bore the appearance of a city. The following day,

Monday, May 7, AD 31, Jesus continued teaching at the same place as yesterday. The Rechabites spoke with Jesus of Malachi, for whom they entertained great veneration. They told Jesus that they esteemed him an angel of God, that he had come as a child to certain pious people, that he had frequently disappeared for a time, and that no one knew whether he was now really dead or not. They dwelt at length on his prophecies of the messiah and his new sacrifice, which Jesus explained as relating to the present and the near future.

Two months later, on Tuesday, July 3, AD 31, in Nobah, Jesus healed many people who were possessed. Outside the pagan quarter of the city dwelt a colony of sincere Rechabites. On their return from the Babylonian captivity they found their city in the possession of the pagans, but they retook it and again reestablished themselves in it. They cherished an extraordinary hatred against the Pharisees and Sadducees, whom they shunned as much as possible. They were engaged in cattle raising and led a very strict life. They drank no wine, excepting on certain feast days, and tenaciously held to the letter of the scripture. Jesus admonished them on this point and gave them an instruction on the spirit of the letter. They were very humble and took in good part all that he said. Many were baptized, among them some pagans, and a great number of possessed were delivered from the evil one.

The Karaites

ON the morning of Wednesday, September 27, AD 30, after teaching in the synagogue, Jesus and the disciples left Dion. After that he went with twelve disciples five hours to the south and over the brook that flowed down from the valley of Ephron. One half-hour to the south of this brook lay Jogbeha, a little, unknown place, quite hidden away in a hollow behind a forest. It was founded by a prophet, a spy of Moses and Jethro, whose name sounds like Malachi. He is not however one and the same with the last prophet, Malachi. Jethro, the father-in-law of Moses, employed him as a servant.

Jesus was very graciously received in the isolated city of Jogbeha. Living apart from the other inhabitants was a sect called Karaites. They wore long, yellow scapulars, white garments, and aprons of rough skin. The youths wore shorter clothes and had their limbs wound with strips of stuff. There were about four hundred of these men. Once upon a time they were of far more importance, but suffered much from the oppression of enemies. They were of the race of Ezra and a descendant of Jethro. One of their teachers had a great dispute once with a distinguished pharisaical doctor. They clung strictly to the letter of the law and rejected oral additions, led a life very simple and plain, and had all their goods in common. If a member withdrew from the community, he had to abandon whatever goods or property he had brought to it. There were no poor among them, for they mutually assisted one another; even strangers were supported by them. They reverenced old age, and among them were many aged persons, whom the young treated with the greatest deference. They called those holding a distinguished position "ancients."

The Karaites were sworn enemies of the Pharisees, who added all sorts of oral traditions to the law, though in some points they were somewhat similar to the Sadducees. In their manners and customs, however, they were different, being far stricter. One of them belonging to this place had married a woman of the tribe of Benjamin and on that account had been driven from the community. It was at the time of the great strife with that tribe. They suffered nothing in the least resembling an image, and they believed that the souls of the deceased passed into other bodies, even into those of the lower animals. They delighted in the thought of the beautiful animals in paradise. They were in expectation of the messiah, after whom they earnestly prayed, but they looked for him to come as a worldly monarch. They regarded Jesus as a prophet. They observed great cleanliness but did not adhere to the numerous purifications, the throwing away of dishes and similar annoying observances not in the law. They followed the law religiously, though interpreting it much more freely than did the Pharisees.

They lived here quietly, having little communication with other people, permitting neither luxury nor vanity, and supporting themselves by their modest labor. A great many willow trees grew in these parts, from which they wove baskets and beehives, for there were many bees around here. They also made coarse covers and light wooden vessels, all working together under long tents. Their arbors for the feast of Tabernacles now at hand stood already prepared outside the city. They entertained Jesus with honey and bread baked in the ashes. Jesus taught here. He instructed them in all things, and they listened to him very reverently. He expressed to them the wish that they should live in Judea, and praised the reverence of their children toward their parents, of the scholars for their teachers, and the regard they entertained for age. He also commended their attention to the poor and the sick, for whom they provided in well-arranged hospitals.

The Ark of the Covenant
and the
Mystery of the Promise

Moses and Joshua in the Tabernacle with the Ark

The Ark of the Covenant
and the Mystery of the Promise

The Promise of the Redeemer

AFTER the fall of humankind, as has been said, God made known to the angels his plan for the restoration of the human race.[1] I saw the throne of God. I saw the Holy Trinity and a movement in the divine Persons. I saw the nine choirs of angels and God announcing to them the way by which He would restore the fallen race. I saw the inexpressible joy and jubilation of the angels at the announcement.

I saw Adam's glittering rock of precious stones arise before the throne of God, as if borne up by angels. It had steps cut in it, it increased in size, it became a throne, a tower, and it extended on all sides until it embraced all things. I saw the nine choirs of angels around it, and above the angels in heaven I saw the image of the Virgin. It was not Mary in time; it was Mary in eternity, Mary in God.[2] The Virgin entered the tower, which opened to receive her, and she appeared to become one with it. Then I saw issuing from the Holy Trinity an apparition which, likewise, went into the tower.

Among the angels I noticed a kind of monstrance at which all were working. It was in shape like a tower, and on it were all kinds of mysterious carving. Near it on either side stood two figures, their joined hands embracing it. At every instant it became larger and more magnificent. I saw Something from God passing

---

[1] To provide a sequential account of the story of the Ark (or Arks) of the Covenant, we commence here with an abridgement of relevant portions of "The Promise of the Redeemer" in *First Beginnings*; and as will be noted below, similar abridgements have been provided for relevant portions drawn from "Abraham" and "Moses."

[2] See "The Eternal Mary" in *The Life of the Virgin Mary*.

through the angelic choirs and going into the monstrance. It was a shining Holy Thing, and it became more clearly defined the nearer it drew to the monstrance. It appeared to me to be the Germ of the divine Blessing for a pure offspring which had been given to Adam but withdrawn when he was on the point of hearkening to Eve and consenting to eat the forbidden fruit. It was the Blessing that was again bestowed upon Abraham, then withdrawn from Jacob, by Moses deposited in the Ark of the Covenant, and, lastly, received by Joachim, the father of Mary, in order that Mary might be as pure and stainless in her conception as was Eve upon coming forth from the side of the sleeping Adam.[1] The monstrance, likewise, went into the tower.

While in Egypt and imprisoned, Joseph received It from an angel. Joseph became a helper, a deliverer of his family, in whom was unending Blessing—both spiritual and corporeal Blessing. As the dying Jacob blessed his children, he set Joseph apart from all the others, saying to him, "The God of your father will be your Helper, and the Almighty will bless you with the blessings of heaven above and with the blessings of the abyss below, with the blessings of the breasts and body of the Mother. Your father's Blessing shall surpass the Blessing of his father, up to the utmost bound of the everlasting hills. It shall come over the head of Joseph, the one among his brothers who is consecrated by God.[2]

As Joseph lay dying, his people were made to swear an oath that his bones would be carried with them when they would leave Egypt for the promised land.

In due course Moses and Aaron fulfilled this oath, for they did take with them upon their departure the bones and other remains of Joseph and Asenath, which were placed in a chest as a Sacred Thing for the whole people—for they knew that Joseph had borne the Blessing.

On Sinai, God gave His people the law, and the tablets of the law; and to Moses was given the task of constructing the Ark of

---

[1] At that time the patriarchs were *themselves* the Ark of the Covenant; *within them* was the Holy Thing, the Blessing, whence the Holy Virgin would one day be born.

[2] Cp. Genesis 49:22–26.

the Covenant,[1] in which would be preserved the Promise, and the tablets, from which God spoke with the people.

Lastly, I saw the Promise received by Joachim, the father of Mary, in order that Mary might be as pure and stainless in her conception as was Eve upon her coming forth from the side of the sleeping Adam.

I saw too a chalice prepared by the angels. It was of the same shape as that used at the Last Supper, and it also passed into the tower. To the right of the tower I saw, as though on the rim of a golden cloud, grapevines and wheat intertwining like the fingers of clasped hands. From them sprang forth a branch—a whole genealogical tree—upon whose boughs were little figures of males and females reaching out their hands to one another. And its uppermost blossom was the crib with the child.

Then I saw in pictures the mystery of redemption, from the Promise down to the fullness of time, and in side pictures I saw *countervailing influences* at work. At last, over the shining rock, I saw a large and magnificent church. It was the one, holy Catholic Church, which bears living in itself the salvation of the whole world. The connection of these pictures one with another, and their transition from one to another, was wonderful. Even what was evil and opposed to the end in view, even what was rejected by the angels as unfit, was made subservient to the unfolding of redemption. And then I saw the ancient temple rising from below. It was very large and like a church—but it had no tower. It was pushed to one side by the angels, and there it stood, slanting. I saw a great mussel shell appear and try to force its way into the old temple; but it too was hurried aside.

I saw a broad, lopped-off tower, through whose numerous gateways figures like Abraham and the children of Israel entered —it was significant of their bondage in Egypt. It too was shoved aside, as well as another Egyptian tower in staircase form. The latter was symbolical of astrology and soothsaying. Then appeared

---

[1] "The chest in which the sacrament was carried after Moses had received it on the night before the Exodus began was small and unexceptional, and bore within stone vessels containing relics of the family of Jacob and Joseph."

an Egyptian temple. It was pushed aside like the others and remained standing, crooked.

At last I saw a vision on earth such as God had shown to Adam—that is, that a Virgin would arise and restore to him the salvation he had forfeited. Adam knew not when it would take place, and I saw his deep sadness, because Eve bore him only sons. But at last she bore a daughter.

I saw Noah and his sacrifice at the time in which he received from God the Blessing. Then I had visions of Abraham, of his Blessing, and of the Promise of a son Isaac. I saw the Blessing descending from firstborn to firstborn, and always transmitted with a sacramental action. I saw Moses on the night of Israel's departure from Egypt getting possession of the Mystery, the Holy Thing, of which no other knew save Aaron. I saw it afterward in the Ark of the Covenant. Only the high priests and certain saints, by a revelation from God, had any knowledge of it. I saw the transmitting of this Mystery through the ancestry of Jesus Christ down to Joachim and Anne, the purest and holiest couple that ever existed, and from whom was born Mary, the spotless Virgin. And then I saw Mary becoming the *living* Ark of God's Covenant.

I saw Melchizedek take possession of many parts of Palestine by marking them off. He measured off the site for the pool of Bethesda, and long before Jerusalem existed he set a stone where the Temple was to stand. I saw him planting in the bed of the Jordan the twelve precious stones upon which the priests stood with the Ark of the Covenant at the departure of the children of Israel. He planted them like seeds, and they increased in size.[1]

Abraham Receives the
Sacrament of the Old Covenant

ABRAHAM sat in front of his tent under a large tree by the roadside.[2] He was in prayer. He often sat thus, waiting to show hospitality to travelers. As he prayed he raised his eyes to heaven and

[1] For a complete account of Melchizedek and his connection with the Ark of the Covenant, see "Melchizedek" in *First Beginnings*.
[2] This section is an abbreviation of the connection of Abraham with the

saw, as in a sunbeam, an apparition from God that announced to him the coming of the three whitish men. He arose and sacrificed a lamb on the altar, before which I saw him kneeling in ecstasy, begging for the redemption of humankind. The altar stood to the right of the large tree, in a tent open above. Further on was a second tent, in which were kept vessels and other utensils for sacrifice. It was to this last that Abraham generally retired when superintending the shepherds who dwelt around here.[1] Still further on, and on the opposite side of the road, was the tent of Sarah and her household. The females always lived apart.

Abraham's sacrifice was almost accomplished when he beheld the three angels appear on the highroad. On they came in their girded garments, one after another, an even distance between them. Abraham hurried out to meet them. Bowing low before God, he saluted them and led them to the tent of the altar. Here they let down their garments and commanded Abraham to kneel.

I saw the wonderful things that now happened to Abraham through the ministry of the angels. He was in ecstasy, and all the actions were rapid, as is usual in such states. I heard the first angel announce to Abraham as he knelt that God would bring forth from his posterity a sinless, an immaculate, maiden who, while remaining an inviolate Virgin, should be the mother of the Redeemer, and that he was now to receive what Adam had lost through sin. Then the angel offered him a shining morsel and made him drink a luminous fluid from a small cup. After that he blessed him, drawing his right hand in a straight line down from Abraham's forehead, then from the right and the left shoulder respectively down under the breast, where the three lines of the blessing united. Then with both hands the angel held something like a little luminous cloud toward Abraham's breast. I saw it entering into him, and I felt as if he were receiving the blessed sacrament.

Ark of the Covenant as more fully described in "Abraham" in *First Beginnings* but here revisited to better follow the story of the Ark of the Covenant, of the Promise, Mystery, Sacrament, or Holy Thing.

[1] See "Abraham" (as above) for a drawing of this scene taken from Brentano's notes.

The second angel told Abraham that he should, before his death, impart the mystery of this Blessing to Sarah's firstborn in the same way he had himself received it. He informed him also that his future grandson, Jacob, would be father to twelve sons, from whom twelve tribes should spring. The angel told him also that this Blessing would be withdrawn from Jacob, but that after Jacob had become a nation it would be restored and placed in the Ark of the Covenant as a Holy Thing belonging to that whole nation. It should be theirs for as long as they gave themselves to prayer. The angel explained to Abraham that on account of the wickedness of men the Mystery would be removed from the Ark and confided to the patriarchs, and that at last it would be given over to a man [Joachim] who would be the father of the promised Virgin. I heard also that, by six prophetesses and through star pictures, it had been made known to the pagans also that the redemption of the world should be accomplished through a Virgin. All this was made known to Abraham in vision, and he saw the Virgin appear in the heavens, an angel hovering at her right and touching her lips with a branch. From the mantle of the Virgin issued the Church.

The third angel foretold to Abraham the birth of Isaac. I saw Abraham so full of joy over the promised Holy Virgin and the vision he had had of her that he gave no thought to Isaac, and I think that this same Promise made the command he subsequently received to sacrifice Isaac easier for him.

After these holy communications I saw how, when Abraham awoke from ecstasy, he led the angels under the tree and placed stools around it. The angels sat down and he washed their feet. Then Abraham hurried to Sarah's tent to tell her to prepare a meal for his guests. This she did and, veiling herself, carried it halfway to them. The meal over, Abraham accompanied the angels a short distance on their journey. It was then that Sarah heard them speak to him of the birth of a son—she had approached them behind the enclosure of the tent. She laughed.[1] I saw numbers of doves tame as hens before the tents. The meal consisted of the same kind of birds, round loaves, and honey. I saw Abraham

---

[1] Genesis 18:12.

escorting the angels at their departure and heard him supplicating for Sodom.

Abraham, at his departure from Chaldea, had already received the mystery of the Blessing from an angel, but it was given him then in a veiled manner and was more like a pledge of the fulfillment of the Promise that he should be the father of an innumerable people. Now, however, the Mystery was resuscitated in him by the angels, and he was enlightened upon it.

The Ark of the Covenant and Moses

ON the same night that Moses took possession of the Holy Thing, a golden casket shaped like a coffin was prepared in which the Israelites carried it upon their departure.[1] It must have been large enough for a man to rest in, for it was to become a Church, a Body. This was the night upon which the doorposts were marked with blood. As I witnessed the rapid building of the chest I thought of the holy cross which, too, was hurriedly joined together on the night before the death of Jesus. The chest was of gold plate and shaped like an Egyptian mummiform coffin, broad above and narrow below. On its upper part was a picture of a face surrounded by beams. On the sides were marked the length of the arms and the position of the ribs. In the center of this coffin-like chest was placed a little golden casket wherein was contained the actual Holy Thing of the Ark—the Sacrament and Promise of the Old Covenant—which Segola had retrieved from the sepulchral vault.[2] Truly, the entire figure was filled with holy objects— for instance, a vessel containing manna rested in a depression at the breast. In the lower part of the chest were sacred vessels, among them the chalice[3] and cups of the patriarchs, which Abra-

---

[1] This also is an abbreviation of the full account of Moses in connection with the Ark of the Covenant, as given in "Moses," in order that the reader may better follow the thread of the story of the Ark in a connected account.

[2] See "Moses," "Segola," also "Joseph and Asenath."

[3] Anne Catherine added that this small chalice might well have been the same the angel gave to Joachim, wherefrom to drink; and also that the anointing oil may have been therein.

ham had received from Melchizedek and which, with the Blessing, had been entailed upon the firstborn.

At the lower, narrower end of the casket, or at the foot of the figure, was Aaron's rod, along with another formed into several longer and shorter gilded tubes—rather in the shape of radiating beams of light. On Aaron's rod were seven buds. It seemed to me that these may have represented the seven gifts of the Holy Spirit.

This was the first form of the Ark of the Covenant, and these its first contents. It had two covers—the lower red, the upper white.

Only afterward, on Mount Sinai, was made the chest inlaid with gold inside and out, into which the golden mummiform coffin with the Holy Thing was placed. The coffin did not fill the chest. It reached only about halfway up, nor was it overlong, for at the head and foot room remained for two small compartments in which were placed relics of Jacob's and Joseph's family, and later on the rod of Aaron. When the Ark of the Covenant was placed in the Temple upon Zion its interior had undergone a change. The golden mummiform coffin had by then been removed and in its place was a little mass of whitish substance shaped like the coffin.

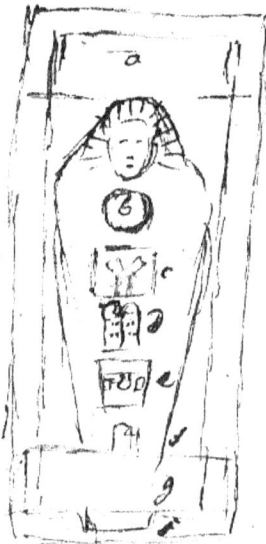

a: Small compartment, above

b: Vessel containing manna, below

c: Casket holding the Mystery (Holy Thing), below

d: Tablets of the Law, above

e: Chest with the mystical chalice and cups

f: Space for Aaron's rod

g: Small compartment below

The upper surface of the figure was slightly vaulted.

The Idol Broken Down Before the Ark

The Ark Passes Over the Jordan

Even as a child I often beheld the Ark of the Covenant. I saw its inside and outside and I knew of all that was placed into it from time to time. All the precious, holy things that the Israelites preserved were kept therein, but it could not have been heavy, for it was readily carried. The chest was longer than broad, and its height equal to its width.[1] It had below a projecting ledge. The upper third of the top—that is, for about two feet—was wrought skillfully in gold: flowers, scrolls, faces, suns, and stars, all in different colors. It was magnificent, although the ornamentation was not very much raised. The apex and leaves rose but slightly above the top of the chest. At the corners below this border, at either end, were two rings through which ran bars for carrying it. The whole chest was of setim (acacia) wood and covered, as has been said, with gold and beautifully inlaid with figures of different colors.

In the middle of the Ark were small, nearly unnoticeable doors, by which the high priest, when alone in the most holy, could take out the Holy Thing for blessing, or for prophesying. The pair of doors, right and left, opened to the interior, providing enough access to admit of the high priest's reaching easily in. Where the bars for carrying it extended over these doors they were slightly curved. When the doors were opened, the golden casket—in which was preserved the Holy Thing in its precious coverings—could be opened like a book.[2] The Holy Thing was taken out by

---

[1] Here is added in parenthesis in the notes: "The Ark of the Covenant was two and a half ells long and one and a half ells in height and width. The upper third of the top was therefore half an ell high."

[2] Brentano summarizes Anne Catherine's words as follows, adding that he was not entirely certain regarding them: "When the Turks opened the side of the Ark, the casket [within] opened like a book. On the two sides were the tablets of the law, and between them the Holy Thing, which she described, as she has done before, as shaped like two beans. Earlier she had also described it as in the form of a Y.

"She once heard someone making light of a Muslim saying, according to which God bequeathed to Adam the Ark of the Covenant already in a finished state, after which it was passed on from one patriarch to the next until finally it came to Moses—and that later, not only were the tablets of the law placed therein but also the sandals (recalling also the shape of beans) that Moses had

the high priests not only on certain occasions for the purpose of prophesying, but also, in rare and very mysterious instances, they would take hold of it with their bare hands—though if they were themselves not of the highest purity they would immediately fall dead. It had a form like the letter Y, or of a wine press,[1] such as in vision I have often seen the cross, as also in the enclosed garden in the Chaldean temple of the pagans.[2]

Above the top of the Ark arose the throne of grace. It consisted of a hollow table covered with gold-plate, within which lay holy bones (perhaps those of Joseph). It was as large as the roof of the Ark but only deep enough to rise a little above it. It was fastened to the Ark by eight setim wood screws, four at either end. It did not rest exactly on the Ark; there was space enough between them to afford a line of sight from side to side. The heads of the screws were of gold and shaped like fruit. The four outer ones fastened the table to the four corners of the Ark, the four inner ones ran into the interior.

Each end of the throne of grace was concave, and in each cavity was securely fastened a golden cherub about the size of a boy. In the center of the throne was a round opening by which a tube

---

been instructed to remove as he stood before the burning bush (Exodus 3:5)." Regarding this account Anne Catherine told the pilgrim: "Yes, I see the Holy Thing, when in the possession of the patriarchs, in the same form as when Abraham received it from the angel—a radiating shape like that of a seed or bean, the two parts thereof curved on one side, for I see the Blessing as twofold."

[1] Wine presses of Anne Catherine's region and time often had an arm or lever that was screwed down as part of the pressing action. To strengthen it, this arm often took the form of a Y, thus providing for two points of contact to distribute the force. On a less mechanical note, an analogy between the winepress and the crucifixion is several times reported in the visions, as also that the cross was formed above in the shape of a Y.

[2] Anne Catherine often described the Holy Thing as living, growing, withering, etc.

ran through the roof of the Ark. One could see it in the space between the roof and the hollow table. This basket-shaped opening was surrounded by a golden crown. Four transverse pieces fastened the crown to the rod, which from the Holy Thing in the Ark arose through the tube and the crown and, like the petals of a flower, spread out into seven points. The right hand of one of the cherubs and the left of the other clasped the rod, while their outspread wings, the right of the one and the left of the other, met behind it. The two other wings, only slightly expanded, did not meet, but left the sight of the crown from the front of the Ark free.

Under these wings the cherubs extended their arms with warning hands. One knee only of each cherub touched the Ark; the other limb was in a hovering attitude. The cherubs turned their faces a little to one side with a slightly agitated expression, as if they felt a holy awe before the radiant crown. They were clothed around the middle portions of the body only. On long journeys they were removed and carried separately in a chest on the back of a camel. I saw on the petal-like points of the rod flames burning, which had been enkindled by the priests. The substance used for these lights was brown. I think it was a sacred resin. They kept it in boxes. But I have often seen great streams of light shooting up out of the crown and similar streams descending from heaven into it, as also oblique currents breaking out of it in fine rays. These last signified the route by which the people should journey. On the lower end of the rod, inside the Ark, were hooks from which hung the two tablets of the law, and below them the Holy Thing. Below the latter, in turn—though not resting on the floor of the Ark—was a ribbed vessel of gold containing manna. When I looked sidewise into the Ark I could not see the altar, nor the Holy Thing.

I always regarded the Ark of the Covenant as a church; the Holy Thing as the altar with the most blessed sacrament; and the vessel of manna as the lamp before the altar.[1] When I entered a church in my childhood, I used to associate its different parts with the corresponding parts of the Ark of the Covenant. The Mystery, the Holy Thing of the Ark, was to me what the blessed sacrament is to us, only not so full of grace—although it was something full of strength and reality. It made upon me a more obscure, a more awe-inspiring impression, but still one very sacred and full of mystery. It always seemed to me that all in the Ark of the Covenant was holy, that all our salvation was in it, as if rolled up in a ball, in a Germ.

When the Ark was opened for special occasions, the cover at the narrow end was raised up, and by this means also the figure within. Three priests were present at such times. The Ark could also be opened from all four sides, and if one looked down into the opening at the lower end, all was as a church.[2]

Moses and Aaron took possession of this holiest Mystery from the grave of Joseph and Asenath on the night before the Exodus out of Egypt, for now, finally—with the latters' bones in hand— they found the strength necessary to commence the journey, whereas previously they had always wavered. That same night, after receiving the Holy Thing, I watched as they built a casket to bear it with them on their journey.

The Holy Thing of the Ark was more mysterious than the most blessed sacrament. The former seemed to be the Germ of the latter; the latter, the fulfillment of the former. I cannot express it.

---

[1] "I compared the vessel of manna, which hung before it, with the eternal lamp, but I found it strange that it was never lit, and also that on account of its size it concealed from view the altar below it."

[2] Anne Catherine had said something to this effect already on an earlier occasion, and she most probably felt this in a deeper sense, according to the mystical arrangements of the Holy Things within the Ark. There is space left in the notes for some further explanation of this enigmatic statement, but unfortunately none is given.

The Holy Thing of the Ark was a Mystery as hidden (to the Jews) as is the Mystery of Jesus in the most holy sacrament hidden to us. I felt that only a few of the high priests knew what it was, that only the pious among them knew it by divine enlightenment and made use of it. To many it was unknown, and so profited them nothing—just as, with us, so many graces and wonders of the Church pass us by unheeded. They are lost, as would be all salvation also, were it founded on human will and intellect instead of upon a rock.

I could weep over the sad state, the blindness, of the Jews. They once possessed all in the Germ; but the fruit they would not recognize. First they had the Mystery, the Holy Thing—it was the pledge, the promise. Then came the law, and afterward the grace. When I saw the Lord teaching in Sichar, the people questioned him as to what had become of the Holy Thing of the Ark of the Covenant. He answered them that humankind had already received a great deal of it, that it was even then among them. The fact of their no longer possessing it as they once did, he said, was a proof that the messiah was born.[1]

How often have I not thought there must be some venerable, deeply-reflective Jews with an inkling of the Holy Thing—if only from tradition, or from ancient, illuminated sages! For did not the Holy Thing in the Ark of the Covenant once reside in the Temple itself? If, in reading holy scripture, we do not glide superficially over its words, but read "through" them—truly behold them—how many profound indications of the Mystery would we not find! But alas, the reality of the Holy Thing slipped away from the Jews in the same way the inner light may be so lost to human souls that they no longer discern the truth in the very written words before them. Had the Church no priestly ordination, no unbroken chain of the laying-on of hands[2] from Christ Jesus to the present, no offering of the New Covenant—had we not all these things, we would possess no more than a general teaching regarding the sacrament of the New Covenant, but not Christ Jesus himself in his flesh and blood, his divinity and his humanity,

[1] See below entry for Sunday, August 31, AD 32.
[2] This is the precise meaning of "tradition," that is, a "handing-on."

as present in the bread and wine of his sacrifice, offered to us for our adoration and sustenance, which alone gives eternal life.

I saw the Mystery, the Holy Thing, in a form—in a kind of veil—as a substance, as an essence, as strength. It was bread and wine, flesh and blood; it was the Germ of the Blessing before the fall. It was the sacramental presence of that holy propagation of humankind before the fall. It was preserved to humankind by religion. It was possible for it to be ever more and more realized in subsequent generations by a continuous purification through piety, which purification was perfected in Mary, thus rendering her fit to receive, through the Holy Spirit, the long-awaited messiah. Noah, in planting the vineyard, had made the preparation; but here, in the Holy Thing, were contained already the reconciliation and protection. Abraham had received it in that Blessing I saw bestowed upon him as something tangible, as a substance. It was a mystery entrusted to one family, therefore the great prerogative of the firstborn.

Before the departure from Egypt, Moses took possession of the Holy Thing. As before this it had been the religious mystery of one family, so now it became the mystery of the whole nation. It was placed in the Ark of the Covenant as the most holy sacrament in the tabernacle and in the monstrance.

When later the children of Israel worshipped the golden calf and fell into gross errors, Moses doubted the power of the Holy Thing. For this he was punished by not being allowed to enter into the promised land. When the Ark fell into the hands of the enemy, the Holy Thing—the bond of union among the Israelites—was removed by the high priest, as was always done when danger threatened. And yet was the Ark still so sacred that the enemy, under the pressure of God's chastising anger, was forced to restore it.

Few comprehended the Holy Thing or the influence it exerted.[1] It often happened that one man by his sins could interrupt

---

[1] "It was lost to the Jews, or disappeared from among them, on account of the many high priests who followed new fashions and so grew in godlessness, for they scarcely knew any longer what it was or how to work with it. Through

the stream of grace, could break the direct genealogical line that was to end in the Savior—or rather, end in the pure vessel that was to receive him from God. In this way was the redemption of the human race long delayed. But penance could again restore continuity to that line. I do not know for certain whether this sacrament was in itself divine, whether it came forth simply and purely as what it was directly from God, or whether it owed its sacred character to a kind of priestly, supernatural consecration. I think, however, that the first proposition is the true one, for I know of a certainty that priests often opposed its action and thus retarded redemption. But they were heavily punished for it, yes, oftentimes even with death itself. When the Holy Thing operated, when prayer was heard, it became bright and increased in size, shining through its covering with a reddish glow. The Blessing proceeding from it would increase or diminish at different times according to the purity and piety of humankind. By prayer, sacrifice, and penance, it appeared to grow larger.

I saw Moses expose it before the people only twice: at the passage through the Red Sea and at the worshipping of the golden calf, but it was covered even then. It was removed from the golden casket and veiled, as is the blessed sacrament on Good Friday. Like it, it was carried before the breast or raised up for a blessing or a malediction as if exerting its influence even at a distance. By it, Moses restrained many of the Israelites from idolatry, and preserved them from death.

The Holy Thing always seemed to me the sacrament of the Old Testament, and as though the whole salvation of humankind was wound up within it as in a coil; for it was not salvation itself, but salvation-in-the-making, the seed of the Promise. It was infinitely holy, but to me seemed sterner, more earnest—even fearsome— than the holy sacrament. It was the grace and salvation of the

such godlessness, and their quibbling and hypocrisy, many sects were robbed of grace, in like manner as grace, and so holiness of other kinds, have often been lost to the people through false teaching and worldly life. And yet do I see the whole treasury of grace and salvation nonetheless preserved in the Church, for she was built by Christ upon a rock and not upon the will, the intellect, or the knowledge of humankind only."

New Testament (nested) in the maternal body of the Old Testament. There was a twofoldness in it, like unto that of man and woman, flesh and blood, wine and wheat. Holy souls of Israel received blessings from the Holy Thing, for example Hannah, the mother of Samuel, who prayed before it in Shiloh, and also Joachim, when the Holy Virgin was promised him, and Zechariah, when his son John the Baptist was promised him.

I often saw the high priest making use of it when alone in the holy of holies. Placing it on a golden platter concealed with the Ark, he would turn it in a certain direction as if to strengthen, to protect, to shield, sometimes to shower a blessing, to grant a petition, sometimes even to punish. He never touched it with uncovered hands.[1] The Holy Thing was also plunged by him into water. This he did with a religious intention, and the water was then given as a sacred draught.[2] Deborah the prophetess, Hannah the mother of Samuel in Shiloh, and Emerentia the mother of Anne drank of this water. By this holy drink was Emerentia prepared for the conception of Anne. Anne drank not of this water, for the Blessing was already in her. Joachim, through an angel, received the Holy Thing out of the Ark of the Covenant, and Mary was conceived under the golden gate of the Temple. And so, at her birth, Mary herself became the Ark of the Holy Thing—which then came to term—and the wooden Ark in the Temple was deprived of its Presence.

When Joachim and Anne met under the golden gate they were surrounded by dazzling light as the Blessed Virgin was conceived without original sin. A wonderful sound was heard, like a voice

---

[1] Elsewhere in this article, however, Anne Catherine says there were rare, mysterious occasions when the high priest *did* take the Holy Thing in his bare hands, adding, however, that this led to the priest's death if he were of insufficient purity in comportment of body and soul.

[2] Anne Catherine says elsewhere: "The high priests took something from the Ark and used it in connection with drinking a water." Brentano adds in a note that most likely this was done at weddings and helped explain the holiness of the firstborn. Elsewhere, again, reference is made to a connection with the uncommon "multiplication" of the nation of Israel. See also "Joseph and Asenath" and "Moses."

from God. Humankind cannot comprehend this mystery of Mary's immaculate conception in Anne, therefore is it hidden from them. The ancestors of Jesus received the Germ of the Blessing for the Incarnation of God; but Jesus Christ is himself the sacrament of the New Covenant, the fruit, the fulfillment, of that Blessing, uniting humankind again to God.

By the time it was received by the Holy Virgin, the Blessing had almost entirely exhausted itself, and now the mother of the Savior became herself the Ark of the Covenant. With the birth of Jesus, the Holy Thing (we could say) was no longer housed in the Temple. For a long time I found it inconceivable that the Jews did not notice that the messiah was born, as ought they not have recognized this from the fact that the Holy Thing had been taken away (from the Temple)?[1]

As the messiah approached, the Blessing appeared more and more in the ancestors of the Holy Virgin, so that less and less was heard of miracles worked by the Ark of the Covenant; that is, the sacrament of the Old Covenant waned with the gradual approach of the sacrament of the New Covenant. The grace of the Old Testament was to bring forward, through its Blessing, the flesh and blood of the God-Man; and so, as they drew nigh, the grace waxed in the stem and stock of the Savior and waned in the Holy Thing in the Temple.

At those times when, under the starry heavens, I saw the holy prophets and ancestors of Mary turned toward the Temple in Jerusalem in endless longing, like parched deer aching for springs of water; or, in a surge of yearning, ripping open the garments upon their breast and crying to the heavens, "O heaven above, send down Thy dew; O clouds, rain down the Righteous One; O earth, open thyself, that He may spring forth!"—at those times, the Blessing passed more abundantly to the chosen of Israel and turned away from those grown evil or corrupt. Yes, turned away was the very fountainhead of the Blessing, the source that had consecrated the Seed of Abraham, Isaac, Jacob, and Joseph and thereafter become, in the Temple, a wellspring of sanctification,

---

[1] Genesis 49:10.

whence flowed all further fonts and springs that God ordained for His people. It was as though the spring of grace, which was the Old Covenant, over time ran dry; and from a new and pure spring was quickened the seed of the nearer forebears of the Holy Virgin—she, the garden meant to blossom from the root of Jesse.

Because the descendents of the patriarchs had become a nation, the Blessing bestowed by God upon the patriarchs of the Old Covenant passed into the Temple, and thence into the patriarchs of the New Covenant, whereafter it began to flourish in the Ark of the New Covenant, that is, the Holy Virgin, who, full of grace and overshadowed by the Holy Spirit, became mother of the Redeemer—who sacrificed himself, his flesh and blood, as God and man, in the holy sacrament of the Church of the New Covenant. Then was the Old Temple broken asunder and the New Temple raised, wherein we worship the Most Holy, by Whom we are nourished unto eternal life. *Pange lingua gloriosi corporis mysterium!* ("Sing, my tongue, the Mystery of the Body Glorious!")[1] Those who fully comprehend this hymn of praise feel the mercy that God bestows upon humankind from the beginning unto eternity.

When Jeremiah at the time of the Babylonian captivity hid the Ark of the Covenant and other precious objects on Mount Sinai, the Mystery, the Holy Thing, was no longer in it; only its coverings did he bury with the Ark. But he knew what it had contained, and how holy it was. He wanted therefore to speak of it publicly and of the abomination of treating it irreverently. But Malachi[2] restrained him and took charge of the Holy Thing himself. Through him it came into the hands of the Essenes, and afterward was placed by a priest in the second Ark of the Covenant.

---

[1] With these words commences a medieval Latin hymn written by St. Thomas Aquinas (1224–1274) for the feast of Corpus Christi, which is also sung on Maundy Thursday during the procession from the church to the place where the blessed sacrament is kept until Good Friday.

[2] "Malachi was, like Melchizedek (as has been said before), an angel, one sent by God. I saw him not as an ordinary man. As with Melchizedek, he had the appearance of a man, differing from Melchizedek only inasmuch as was suited to his time." See "Malachi."

Shortly after Daniel was led to Babylon, I saw Malachi as a lad of seven years, wearing a reddish garment and wandering around with a staff in his hand. He seemed to have lost his way and took shelter at Sapha with a pious couple of the tribe of Zebulon. They thought him a lost child of one of the captive Israelites and kept him with them. He was very amiable, and so uncommonly patient and meek that he was loved by all—and so, without molestation, could teach and do what else he pleased. He had much contact with Jeremiah, whom he assisted with advice when in the greatest perils. Through his doings also was Jeremiah freed from prison in Jerusalem. The Ancient Ark of the Covenant, hidden by Jeremiah on Mount Sinai, was never again discovered. The second one was not so beautiful as the first, nor did it contain as many precious things. Aaron's rod was at that time in the possession of the Essenes on Mount Horeb, where was preserved also a part of the Holy Thing.[1] The family Moses appointed as immediate protectors of the Ark of the Covenant existed till the time of Herod.

All will come to light on the Last Day. Then will the Mystery come clear, to the terror of all who have made bad use of it.

---

[1] In this connection we read elsewhere in Brentano's notes that the Holy Thing did not remain in this figure and in this arrangement in the Ark. Neither was it therein at the time of the Philistine's conquest, for at God's command Samuel had earlier carried it to Mount Hebron. Also, it was altered in its contents and arrangement at the time it was kept in the house of Obed-Edom (Samuel 6:10–11; 1 Chronicles 13:13–14), whence it was later taken to Zion. The larger figure was no longer within the Ark, but instead the Holy Thing was kept in a similar but smaller figure composed of some white substance, and kept erect within a tabernacle set between the two tablets of the law. It was sheathed in some way in gold. This later figure was not well-proportioned, being rather too short for its width. At the time Jeremiah hid the Ark it may have been that the tablets of the law and various other holy objects from the Ark were hidden also; but as for the Holy Thing, it found its place in the New Ark, for the grace proceeding therefrom was palpable to Anne Catherine. This grace came to an end with the conception of Mary, which signified the fulfillment of the whole purpose of the Holy Thing in the Ark. (Nevertheless, as Anne Catherine told it, even after this, Zechariah seemed still to receive a grace of fruitfulness from the Ark.)

The Ark Among the Essenes on Mount Horeb

THE place where the head of the Essenes on Mount Horeb prayed and prophesied was the cave where Elijah had formerly dwelt. Many steps led to it up the mountainside, and one entered the cave through a small, cramped opening, and down a few steps. Here the prophet Archos went in alone. For the Essenes this was as if the high priest in the Temple went into the *sanctissimum*—for this was their holy of holies. Within were several mysterious holy things, difficult to describe. I will tell what I can remember of them.

First, I saw Anne's grandmother seeking counsel from the prophet Archos. She came from Mara in the desert, where her family, which belonged to the married Essenes, owned property. Her name sounded to me like Moruni or Emorun. When the time came for her to be married, she had several suitors, and I saw her go to the prophet Archos on Horeb for him to decide whom she was to accept. She went into a separate part of the large assembly hall and spoke to Archos, who was therein, through a grating, as if she were making her confession to him. It was only in this way that women approached the place. I then saw Archos put on his ceremonial vestments and ascend, thus arrayed, the many steps to the top of the Mount, where he entered the cave of Elijah by the little door and down the steps. Then he shut the door behind him and opened a hole in the vaulting, dimly illuminating the cave, the interior of which had been carefully hollowed out.

Against the wall I saw a small altar carved out of the rock, and noticed, though not quite clearly, several sacred objects on it, among them several pots with low-growing bushes of herbs. They were the herbs that grow as high as the hem of Jesus's garment.[1] I know this herb, for it grows with us, though not so vigorously. The plants gave Archos some sort of indication, in his

---

[1] Anne Catherine unquestionably meant that these herbs were the same as those mentioned by Eusebius in his *Ecclesiastical History,* book VII, chapter 18, which he says grew around the statue of Jesus Christ put up by the woman of Caesarea Philippi who was cured of the issue of blood. The plants acquired the

prophetic knowledge, according to whether they faded or flourished. In the middle between these little bushes of herbs I saw something like a small tree, taller than them, with leaves that looked yellowish and were twisted like snail shells. There seemed to me to be little figures on this tree. I cannot now say for certain whether this tree was living or made by some artifice,[1] like the tree of Jesse. On this small tree with twisted leaves could be seen, as on a tree of Jesse or on a genealogical table, how soon the coming of the Blessed Virgin was to be expected. It looked to me as if it were living, and yet it seemed also to be a receptacle of some kind, for I saw that a blossoming branch was kept inside it. I think it was Aaron's rod, which had once been in the Ark of the Covenant.

When Archos prayed in the cave of Elijah for a revelation on the occasion of a marriage among Mary's ancestors, he took this rod of Aaron into his hand. If the marriage was destined to take its place in the Blessed Virgin's ancestry, the rod put forth a bud that produced one or more flowers, among which single flowers were sometimes marked with the sign of the elect. Certain buds represented particular ancestors of Anne, and when these came to be married, Archos observed the buds in question and uttered his prophecies according to the manner in which they unfolded.

The Essenes of Mount Horeb had, however, another holy relic in the cave of Elijah—nothing less than a part of the Most Holy Mystery of the Ark of the Covenant, which came into their possession when the Ark fell into the hands of enemies.[2] This Holy Thing, concealed in the Ark of the Covenant, was known only to the holiest of the high priests and to a few prophets, but I think I

---

power of healing all kinds of sicknesses as soon as they had grown high enough to touch the hem of the statue's garment. Eusebius says that this plant was of an unknown species. Anne Catherine had spoken before of the statue and of these plants. CB

[1] The German word *Futteral*, here translated as "made by artifice," more specifically has the sense of case, cover, or sheath.

[2] Anne Catherine spoke here uncertainly of a quarrel and schism among the Levites. Then she added: "This part was something like a circumcised fore-

learned it is in some way mentioned in the little-known secret books of the old Jewish thinkers.[1] It was no longer complete in the new Ark of the Covenant in the Temple as restored by Herod. It was no work of human hands, but a mystery, a most holy secret of the divine Blessing on the coming of the Blessed Virgin full of grace, in whom, by the overshadowing of the Holy Spirit, the Word became flesh and God became man.

Before the Babylonian captivity this Holy Thing had been whole in the Ark of the Covenant; I now saw part of it here in the possession of the Essenes. It was kept in a chalice of shining brown, which seemed to be made of a precious stone. They prophesied, too, with the help of this Holy Thing, which seemed sometimes, as described before, to put forth little buds.

I saw that the Essenes on Mount Horeb had in their caves recesses in the walls where bones, carefully wrapped in cotton and silk, were kept as sacred relics behind gratings. They were bones of prophets who had lived here, and also of the children of Israel who had died near here. There were little pots of green plants standing beside them. The Essenes used to light lamps and pray before the bones in veneration of them.

It is remarkable that it was always about female children that these prophets made predictions, and that Anne's ancestors and Anne herself had mostly daughters. It was as if the object of all their devotion and prayers was to obtain from God a blessing on pious mothers from whose descendants the Blessed Virgin, the mother of the Savior himself, should spring, as well as the families of his precursor and of his friends and disciples.

Archos, after entering the cave of Elijah, shut the door and

---

skin, about the length of a finger, which lay in a brownish chalice that shone as though made of precious stones. [This latter] was not made by human hands, but was of a substance like flesh, but full of mystery. It was sometimes used to prophesy." There follows this brief note, followed by a question mark: "On occasion small blossoms appeared upon it." See also "Moses" and "Joseph and Asenath."

[1] In July 1840, some twenty years after this communication, Brentano learned from a language expert that the cabalistic book Zohar contains several references to this matter.

knelt down in prayer. He looked up to the opening in the vaulting and threw himself face downward on the ground. I then saw the prophetic knowledge that was given him. He saw that from under the heart of Emorun, who was seeking his counsel, there grew as it were a rose tree with three branches, a rose on each. The rose on the second branch was marked with a letter, I think an M. He saw still more. An angel wrote letters on the wall. I saw Archos rise up as if awaking and read these letters. I forget the details. He then went down from the cave and announced to the maiden who was awaiting his answer that she was to marry, and that her sixth suitor was to be her husband. She would bear a child marked with a sign, who was chosen out as a vessel of election in preparation for the coming of the Savior.

The Promise and the
Immaculate Conception of Mary

WHEN Joachim approached the Temple, two of the priests came out to meet him. They did this acting upon a divine inspiration. Joachim had brought with him two lambs and three kids. His offering was accepted, slaughtered, and burned at the customary place in the Temple. But a part of it was taken and burned at another place to the right of the entrance porch, in the center of which stood the large teacher's desk.

When the smoke rose I saw a beam of light descend upon Joachim and the officiating priest. There was a pause, the beholders looked on in amazement, and I saw two priests go out to Joachim and lead him through the side apartments into the sanctuary before the altar of incense. Then the priests laid incense upon the altar, not in grains but in the lump; it kindled of itself. The priests immediately retired to a distance and left Joachim alone before the altar. I saw him on his knees, his arms extended, while the incense offering slowly consumed itself. He remained shut up in the Temple all night, praying with great and ardent desires. I saw that he was in ecstasy. A luminous figure appeared to him in the same manner as to Zechariah, and gave him a roll written in shining letters. On it were the three names: Helia, Hannah, and Miriam—and near the last one the picture of a little Ark of the Covenant, or a Tabernacle. Joachim laid the roll on his breast under his garment.

The angel spoke: "Anne will conceive an immaculate child, from whom the Redeemer of the world will be born." The angel told him moreover not to grieve over his sterility, which was not a disgrace to him but a glory, for that what his spouse would conceive should be, not from him, but through him, a fruit from God, the culminating point of the Blessing given to Abraham. I saw that Joachim could not comprehend these words.

The angel now removed something from the Ark of the Covenant, though without opening the door. It was the Mystery of the Ark, the Sacrament of the Incarnation, the Immaculate Conception, the Consummation of the Blessing of Abraham. I beheld it under the appearance of a luminous body. The angel blessed or anointed Joachim's forehead with the tip of his thumb and forefinger; then he slipped the shining body under Joachim's garment and it entered into him, how I cannot say. He also gave him something to drink out of a glittering chalice which he held supported by two fingers. The chalice was of the same shape as that used at the Last Supper, but without a foot. Joachim was directed to take it with him and keep it at his home.

Then the angel led him behind the curtain that concealed the grating before the holy of holies. The space between the curtain and the grating afforded standing room. The angel held up before Joachim's face a shining ball that reflected like a mirror. Joachim breathed upon it and gazed into it. And now, as if called up by Joachim's breath, appeared all kinds of pictures in the globe. He saw them clearly, for his breath did not dim them. It seemed to me that the angel then said to him that Anne should conceive, although remaining just as unsullied by him as this ball. The angel then took it from Joachim and raised it on high. I saw it hovering in the air and, as if through an opening, innumerable and wonderful pictures went into it. They were like a whole world, one picture growing out of another. Up in the highest point appeared the Most Holy Trinity, and below, to one side, were paradise, Adam and Eve, the fall, the Promise of a Redeemer, Noah, his ark, scenes connected with Abraham and Moses, the Ark of the Covenant, and numerous symbols of Mary. I saw cities, towers, gateways, flowers, all wonderfully connected together by beams of light like bridges. They were all assaulted and combated by beasts and spirits, which however were everywhere beaten back by the streams of light that burst upon them. I saw also a garden enclosed by a dense thornhedge. All kinds of horrible animals were trying to enter, but could not. I saw a tower stormed by numerous warriors who were, however, each time repulsed.

In this way I saw innumerable pictures bearing reference to Mary. They were bound together by passages or bridges, as was said. In them I saw obstacles, hindrances, struggles, all of which were overcome, and the pictures disappeared successively on the opposite side of the globe, as if they had entered into the heavenly Jerusalem. But as I gazed at them dissolving in the interior of the globe, the globe itself mounted on high and I saw it no more.

I understood that the angel forbade Joachim to reveal anything about this holy mystery; and then too I understood why Zechariah, the father of the Baptist, was struck mute after receiving the Blessing and the Promise of Elizabeth's fruitfulness through the Mystery of the Ark of the Covenant. Not till later was this Mystery missed from the Ark by the priests. Then were they at first confounded; afterward they became altogether pharisaical.

The angel now led Joachim out of the holy of holies and vanished. Joachim lay on the ground like one stupefied. I saw the priests enter the sanctuary, lead Joachim out reverently, and place him upon a seat that stood on a raised platform where usually only priests sat. The seat was almost like that used by Magdalene in her grandeur. They bathed his face, held something to his nose, and gave him to drink; in short, they treated him as one in a swoon. Joachim was, by virtue of what he had received from the angel, quite radiant. He looked as if he had returned to the bloom of youth.

Joachim was afterward conducted by the priests to the entrance of the subterranean passage that ran beneath the Temple and under the golden gate. This was a passage set aside for special purposes. Under certain circumstances penitents were conducted by it for purification, reconciliation, and absolution. The priests parted from Joachim at the entrance and he went alone into the narrow, gradually widening and almost imperceptibly descending passage. In it stood pillars twined with foliage. They looked like trees and vines, and the green and gold decorations of the walls sparkled in the rosy light that fell from above.

Joachim had accomplished a third part of the way when Anne met him in the center of the passage directly under the golden gate, where stood a pillar like a palm tree with hanging leaves and fruit. Anne had been conducted into the subterranean passage through an entrance at the opposite end by the priest to whom she and her maid had brought an offering of doves in baskets, and to whom also she had told what the angel had revealed to her. She was also accompanied by some women, among them the prophetess Anna.

I saw Joachim and Anne embrace each other in ecstasy. They were surrounded by hosts of angels, some floating over them carrying a luminous tower like that we see in the pictures of the Litany of Loretto. The tower vanished between Joachim and Anne, both of whom were encompassed by brilliant light and glory. At the same moment the heavens above them opened and I saw the joy of the Most Holy Trinity and of the angels over the conception of Mary. Both Joachim and Anne were in a supernatural state. I learned that at the moment in which they embraced and the light shone around them, the immaculate conception of Mary was accomplished. I was also told that Mary was conceived just as conception would have been effected, were it not for the fall of humankind.

The Ark of the Covenant and the Birth of Mary

SEVERAL days prior to Mary's birth, Anne informed Joachim that the time of her delivery was at hand. She sent messengers to her sister Maraha at Sepphoris, also to the widow Enue, Elizabeth's sister, in the valley of Zebulon, and to her sister Sobe's daughter Mary Salome, the wife of Zebedee of Bethsaida. The sons of Mary Salome and Zebedee, James the Greater and John, were not yet born. Anne sent for these three women to come to her. I saw them on their journey. Two of them were accompanied by their husbands, who returned, however, when they had reached the neighborhood of Nazareth.

On the evening before the birth of the child Mary I saw the three women approaching Anne's abode. When they arrived they went straight to her apartment back of the fireplace. Anne embraced them, told them that her time drew near, and, standing, intoned with them a psalm: "Praise God, the Lord. He has had pity on his people and has freed Israel. Truly, he has fulfilled the Promise that he made to Adam in paradise: 'The seed of the woman shall crush the serpent's head.'"

I do not remember all, verse for verse, but Anne rehearsed the different Types of Mary, and said: "The Germ that God gave to Abraham has ripened in me. The Promise made to Sarah, and the blossom of Aaron's rod, are in me fulfilled." During all this time Anne was shining with light. The room was full of glory, and over Anne hovered Jacob's ladder. The women around her were amazed, entranced. I think they too saw the ladder.

And now a slight refreshment was placed before the visitors. They ate and drank standing, and toward midnight lay down to rest. But Anne remained up in prayer. After awhile she went and roused the women. She felt that her time was near and desired them to pray with her. They all withdrew behind a curtain that concealed an oratory. Anne opened the doors of a little closet built into the wall. In it was a box containing sacred treasures, and on either side lights so contrived that they could be raised in their sockets at pleasure, and rested on upright supports. These lamps were now lighted. At the foot of the little altar was a cushioned stool. The box contained some of Sarah's hair, which Anne held in great reverence; some of the bones of Joseph, which Moses had brought with him out of Egypt; something belonging to Tobias, relics of clothing I think; and the little, white, shining, pear-shaped cup from which Abraham drank when he received the Blessing from the angel, and which was later taken from the Ark of the Covenant and given to Joachim along with the Blessing. This Blessing was like wine and bread, like a sacrament, like a supernatural, invigorating food.

Anne knelt before the shrine, one of the women on either side, and the third behind her. Again I heard them reciting a psalm. I think that the burning bush on Horeb was mentioned in it.

And now a supernatural light began to fill the chamber and to hover around Anne. The three women fell prostrate, as if stunned. Around Anne the light took the exact form of the thornbush on Horeb, so that I could no longer see her. The flame streamed inward, and all at once I saw Anne receiving into her arms the shining child Mary. She wrapped it in her mantle, pressed it to her heart, laid it on the stool before the relics, and went on with her prayer.

Then I heard the child crying, and I saw Anne drawing forth some linen from under the large veil that enveloped her. She swathed the child first in gray and then in red, leaving the breast, arms, and head bare, and then the luminous thornbush vanished. The holy women arose and in glad surprise received the newborn child into their arms. They wept for joy. All intoned a hymn of praise while Anne held the child on high. I saw the chamber again filled with light and myriads of angels. They announced the child's name, singing: "On the twentieth day shall this child be called Mary." Then they sang the *Gloria* and *Alleluia*. I heard all these words.

When Mary was born, I saw her at one and the same time before the Most Holy Trinity in heaven and on earth in Anne's arms. I saw the joy of the whole heavenly court. I saw all her gifts and graces in a supernatural way revealed to her. I often have such visions, but they are for me inexpressible and for others unintelligible; therefore am I silent with regard to them. Mary was also instructed in innumerable mysteries. As this vision ended, the child cried upon earth.

The Promise and Preparations
for Mary's Presentation in the Temple

AT last, Mary was blessed by the priests.[1] I saw her radiant with light as she stood on the little altar throne, two priests on either side of her and one opposite. They held rolls of writing and

---

[1] "During these holy ceremonies I beheld Mary becoming at times so tall that she rose even above the heads of the priests. This was for me a sign of her wisdom and grace. The priests were filled with amazement, at once solemn and joyful."

prayed over the child, their hands outstretched above her. At that moment I saw a wonderful vision in the child Mary. She seemed, by virtue of the Blessing, to become transparent. In her was a glory, a halo of unspeakable splendor, and in that halo appeared the Mystery of the Ark of the Covenant, as if in a glittering crystal vessel. I saw Mary's heart open like the doors of a Temple and the Holy Thing of the Ark of the Covenant—around which a tabernacle of precious stones of multiplied signification had been formed like a heavenly throne—going into her heart through that opening like the Ark of the Covenant into the holy of holies, like the monstrance into the tabernacle. I saw that by this the child Mary was glorified; she hovered above the earth. With the entrance of this sacrament into Mary's heart—which immediately closed over it—the vision faded and I saw the child all penetrated by glowing fervor. During this wonderful vision I saw that Zechariah received an interior assurance, a heavenly intimation that Mary was the chosen vessel of the Mystery. From it he had received a ray that had appeared figuratively in Mary.[1]

Later I saw Joachim, Anne, and their elder daughter Mary Heli busied during the night packing and preparing for a journey. A lamp with several wicks was burning, and I saw Mary Heli busily going about with a light. Joachim saddled two of the beasts of burden and loaded them with all kinds of baggage: clothes for the child and presents for the Temple.

Two of the priests were still present. One was very old. He wore a cap pointed on the forehead and with lappets over the ears. His upper garment was shorter than the under one, and over it was a kind of stole. He had much to do with the child. The other priest was younger.

I saw also two boys present. They were not human. They appeared there supernaturally and with a spiritual signification. They carried long standards rolled upon staffs furnished with knobs at both ends. The larger of the two boys came to me with

---

[1] In another place Anne Catherine says: "Zechariah, the father of the Baptist, did not receive the Blessing from the Ark of the Covenant, but from an angel."

his standard unfurled, read, and explained it to me. The writing appeared entirely strange to me, the single, golden letters all inverted. One letter represented a whole word. The language sounded unfamiliar, but I understood it all the same. He showed me in his roll the passage referring to the burning thornbush of Moses. He explained to me how the thornbush burned and yet was not consumed; that so now was the child Mary inflamed with the fire of the Holy Spirit but in her humility knew nothing of it. It signified also the divinity and humanity in Jesus, and how God's fire united with the child Mary.

The putting-off of the shoes[1] he explained thus: "The law will now be fulfilled. The veil is withdrawn and the essence appears." By the little standard on his staff was signified, as he told me, that Mary now began her course, her career, to become the mother of the Redeemer. The other boy seemed to be playing with his standard. He jumped about and ran around with it. By this was signified Mary's innocence. The great Promise is to be fulfilled in her, rests upon her, and yet she plays like a child in this holy destiny. I cannot express the loveliness of those boys.[2] They were different from all others present, and these latter did not appear to see them. The little procession was also accompanied by the other apparitions of the prophets. As Mary hastened from the house, they pointed out to me a place in their rolls wherein it was declared that, although the Temple was indeed magnificent, yet Mary contained in herself still greater magnificence. Mary wore the little yellowish gown and the large veil so fastened around her that her arms could rest in it. When she rode, the prophet boys followed behind her; but when she walked, they were at her side, singing Psalms 44 and 49. I knew that the same would be sung at her reception in the Temple. The child Mary saw those boys, but said nothing about it. She was perfectly silent, wholly recollected in self.

[1] Exodus 3:5.

[2] See "Departure of the Child Mary for the Temple • Two Prophet-Boys" in *The Life of the Virgin Mary*, which includes similar passages, among them these: "Anne Catherine spoke for a long time with childlike delight of these two boys,

The Promise, Mary's Entrance into the Temple, and Her Offering

NOW the priests led the Holy Virgin up a long flight of steps in the wall that separated the sanctuary from the rest of the Temple. They stood her in something like a niche, from which she could see into the Temple, where were ranged numbers of men who seemed to be consecrated to its service. Through an opening contrived for the purpose one could cast incense upon the altar without entering the court. The priest now at the incense altar was a holy old man. While he offered sacrifice and the cloud of incense arose around Mary I saw a vision, which grew in magnitude until at last it filled the whole Temple and obscured it.

but could not clearly say who they really were. After, however, having eaten and then slept for a few minutes, she recollected herself and said: 'It was the spiritual meaning of these boys that I saw; their presence there was not a natural one. They were only the symbolic representations of prophets. The taller of the two—the one who carried his scroll so solemnly—showed me in it the passage in the third chapter of the book of Exodus where Moses sees the Lord in the burning bush and is told to put off his shoes from his feet. He explained this to me: as the bush was on fire without being burnt, so now was the fire of the Holy Spirit burning in the child Mary, who, all unconscious of it, was bearing this holy flame within her. This passage also, he said, foreshadowed the union, now approaching, of the Godhead with humanity. The fire signified God, the thornbush humankind. The boy also explained to me the meaning of the putting off of the shoes, but I have no clear recollection of what he said. I think it signified the removal of the outer covering to disclose the reality within, and foreshadowed the fulfillment of the law and the coming of one greater than Moses and the prophets. The other boy carried his scroll at the end of a thin stick, blowing in the wind like a flag; this signified the joyous entry of Mary on the path that was leading her to her destiny as the mother of the Redeemer. The childish behavior of this boy, as he played with his scroll, showed how Mary—though overshadowed by so great a Promise and called to so holy a destiny—kept all the innocent playfulness of a child. Actually, these boys explained to me *seven* passages out of their scrolls, but in the interruptions and troubles of daily life I have forgotten everything except what I have now told. O my God! all that I see is so beautiful and so deep, so simple and so clear, and yet I cannot tell it properly and cannot help forgetting so much because of the miserable, detestable happenings of this wretched earthly life.'"

145

I saw above the heart of Mary the glory and the mystery of the Ark of the Covenant. At first it looked exactly like the Ark of the Covenant, and lastly like the Temple itself. Out of the Mystery, and before Mary's breast, arose a chalice similar to that of the Last Supper; above it and just in front of her mouth appeared bread marked with a cross. Beams of light radiated around her, and in them shone her various types and symbols. The mysterious pictures of the *Litany of Loretto*, and the other names and titles of Mary, I saw ranged up the whole flight of steps and around her. From her shoulders, right and left, stretched an olive and a cedar branch crosswise above an elegant palm tree with a small tuft of leaves that stood directly behind her. In the intervening spaces of this verdant cross appeared all the instruments of Christ's passion. Over the vision hovered the Holy Spirit, a figure winged with glory, in appearance more human than dove-like.[1]

The heavens opened above Mary and the central point of the heavenly Jerusalem, the City of God, floated over her with all the gardens, the palaces, and the dwellings of the future saints. Angels in myriads hovered around, and the glory that encircled her was full of angelic faces. Ah, who can express it! Infinite variety, unceasing change, all these pictures following quickly upon, and, as it were, growing out, of one another. Innumerable points

---

[1] On another occasion Anne Catherine spoke similarly of forms of the Holy Spirit as follows: "As Jesus stepped out [of the baptismal well] I saw above him a great pathway of light leading up to heaven, in which was also a voice; and in this I saw something like an orb even brighter within, while outwardly raying forth brilliant light of rainbow colors. In its midst I beheld a form with outspread wings. It did not have exactly the form of a dove; neither was its altogether human in shape. It was winged, though, and manifested both uncommon strength and grace. It was far larger than any dove. The form of the being that lowered itself to the pool of Bethesda to stir its waters was more human in appearance than this, though it was still an angel. However, the being that later appeared above those baptized in this same pool of Bethesda at Pentecost was the same I beheld at the baptism of the Lord in the Jordan. I beheld this same form also at the outpouring of the Holy Spirit upon the disciples. Indeed, never did I see Jesus himself baptize, and it seems to me that Baptism first became a sacrament after the feast of Pentecost, when I saw the Holy Spirit descend upon those whom the disciples baptized."

of this vision I have forgotten. All the splendor and magnificence of the Temple, the richly ornamented wall before which Mary was standing—all grew dark and somber. The whole Temple disappeared, for Mary and her glory alone were visible.

In this vision, symbolic of Mary's spiritual signification, I saw her not as a child, but full-grown. She hovered in the air. And through and through the vision I still saw the priests, the incense offering, and everything else. Then the priest at the altar appeared to prophesy and to call upon the people to thank God and to pray, for that great things were to come upon the child. The crowd in the Temple, greatly awed—although they had not seen the vision that I saw—maintained a solemn stillness. The vision faded away just as gradually as it had unfolded. At last, the Mystery of the Ark of the Covenant shone again in its glory over her heart, and the child once more stood there alone in her rich attire.

The Promise and Mary's Visitation

I SAW Zechariah and Joseph spending the night in the garden at some distance from the house. They slept part of the time in the little summer house and prayed during the other part in the open air. They returned quite early in the morning to the house, where Mary and Elizabeth had passed the night. Mary and Elizabeth recited together morning and evening the hymn of thanksgiving, the *Magnificat*, which Mary had received from the Holy Spirit at the salutation of Elizabeth. During its recital they stood opposite each other against the wall, as if in choir, their hands crossed upon their breast, the black veil of each covering her face. At the second part, which refers to God's Promise, I saw the previous history of the most holy incarnation and the mystery of the most holy sacrament of the altar, from Abraham down to Mary. I saw Abraham sacrificing Isaac, also the Mystery of the Ark of the Covenant that Moses received on the night before the departure from Egypt and by which he was enabled to escape and conquer. I recognized its connection with the holy incarnation, and it seemed to me as if this Mystery were now fulfilled or living in Mary.

I saw also the prophet Isaiah and his prophecy of the Virgin, and from him to Mary visions of the approach of the most blessed sacrament. I still remember that I heard the words: "From father to father down to Mary, there are more than fourteen generations." I saw also Mary's blood taking its rise in her ancestors and flowing nearer and nearer to the incarnation. I have no words to describe this clearly. I can say only that I saw, sometimes here, sometimes there, the people of different races. There seemed to issue from them a beam of light that always terminated in Mary as she appeared at that moment with Elizabeth. I saw this beam issuing first from the Mystery of the Ark of the Covenant and ending in Mary. Then I saw Abraham and from him a ray, which again ended in Mary, etc.

Abraham must have dwelt quite near to Mary's abode at that time, for during the *Magnificat* I saw that the beam proceeding from him came from no great distance, while those from persons nearer to the Mother of God in point of time seemed to come from afar. Their rays were as fine, as clear, as those of the sun when they shine through a narrow opening. In such a beam I beheld Mary's blood glancing red and bright, and it was said to me: "Behold, as pure as this red light must the blood of that Virgin be from whom the Son of God will become incarnate."

Jesus Discourses with Eliud the Essene upon the Mysteries of the Old Testament and the Incarnation

ON Wednesday, September 7, AD 29, Jesus passed the whole day in most confidential conversation with Eliud,[1] who asked him various questions about his mission. Jesus explained all to the old man, telling him that he was the messiah, speaking of the lineage of his human genealogy and the mystery of the Ark of the Covenant. I learned then that that Mystery had, before the deluge, been taken into the ark of Noah, that it had descended from generation to generation, disappearing from time to time, but again coming to light. Jesus said that Mary at her birth had become the

---

[1] See "Eliud the Essene" in *People of the New Testament III*.

Ark of the Covenant of the Mystery.[1] Then Eliud who, during the discourse, frequently produced various rolls of writing and pointed out different passages of the prophets—which Jesus then explained to him—asked why he, Jesus, had not come sooner upon earth. Jesus answered that he could have been born only of a woman who had been conceived in the same way that, were it not for the fall, all humankind would have been conceived; and that, since the first parents, no married couple had been so pure, both in themselves and in their ancestors, as Anne and Joachim.

Then Jesus unfolded the past generations to Eliud and pointed out to him the obstacles that had delayed redemption. I learned from this conference many details concerning the Ark of the Covenant. Whenever it was in any danger, or whenever there was fear of its falling into enemies' hands, the Mystery was removed by the priests; yet still was it—the Ark—so holy that its profaners were punished and forced to restore it. I saw that the family to whom Moses entrusted the special guardianship of the Ark existed until Herod's time. At the Babylonian captivity, Jeremiah hid the Ark and other sacred things on Mount Sinai. They were never afterward found, but the Mystery had been removed. A second Ark was at a later period—that of the second Temple—constructed on the model of the First, but it did not contain the sacred objects that had been preserved in the First. Aaron's rod, and also a portion of the Mystery, were in the keeping of the Essenes on Mount Horeb. The sacrament of the Blessing was, however—but I know not by what priest—again replaced in the Ark. In the pit, which was afterward the pool of Bethesda, the sacred fire had been preserved.

---

[1] In Brentano's notes regarding these words spoken to Eliud, we find this remarkable passage, in which Anne Catherine describes her own experience at the commencement of the relevant vision: "Of all the images of the Blessing of the Mystery that I received, I can recall but few. Most wonderful and incomprehensible to me was that, as the pictures came before me, I believed that at some point I was given to imbibe the Holy Thing itself. It was as though in this way my heavenly Bridegroom—indeed all holiness—was in me, grew within me. It was a picture beyond words from the mystery of life. I seemed to hover on a plank between water and land, and could see through all things and mysteries of the world. I strove toward the land, however, and came to a cloister."

I saw in pictures very many things, which Jesus explained to Eliud; and I heard part of the words, but cannot recall all. He related the fact of his having taken flesh of the blessed Germ of which God had deprived Adam before his fall. That blessed Germ, by means of which all Israel should have become worthy of him, had descended through many generations. He explained how his coming had been so often delayed, how some of the chosen vessels had become unworthy. I saw all this as a reality. I saw all the ancestors of Jesus, and how the ancient patriarchs at their death gave over the Blessing sacramentally to the firstborn. I saw that the morsel and the drink out of the holy cup, which Abraham had received from the angel along with the promise of a son, Isaac, were a symbol of the most holy sacrament of the New Covenant, and that their invigorating power was due to the flesh and blood of the future messiah. I saw the ancestors of Jesus receiving this sacrament, in order to contribute to the incarnation of God; and I saw that Jesus, of the flesh and blood received from his forefathers, instituted a most august sacrament for the uniting of humankind with God.[1]

Jesus spoke much to Eliud also of the sanctity of Anne and Joachim, and of the supernatural conception of Mary under the golden gate. He told him that not by Joseph had he been conceived, but from Mary according to the flesh; that she had been conceived of that pure Blessing which had been taken from Adam before the fall, which through Abraham had descended until it

---

[1] This passage is given here again, more literally rendered from the notes, as providing further nuances of meaning: "Jesus took on flesh from this Germ that was taken away from Adam. It had coursed through many lines of descent, often obstructed along its way when vessels meant to receive it had gone dark. Truly did I see all this—I saw the ancestors of Jesus after the flesh, and how before their death the patriarchs, with a sacramental blessing, passed this force on to their firstborn. I saw that the morsel and draught from the small cup that Abraham received from the angel was a prefiguration of the holy sacrament and a strengthening for the future flesh and blood of the messiah. Jesus's lines of descent received this holy sacrament, that God might become man; and that later, as God-Man, he might institute the holy sacrament to unite humankind again with God."

was possessed by Joseph in Egypt, after whose death it had been deposited in the Ark of the Covenant, and thence withdrawn to be handed over to Joachim and Anne.[1] Jesus said that to free humankind he had been sent in the weakness of humanity; that he received and felt everything like a man; that, like the serpent of Moses in the desert, he would one day be raised up on Mount Golgotha, where the body of the first man lay buried. He referred also to the sad future that awaited him and to the ingratitude of humankind.

The want of understanding on the part of those around Jesus is always a subject of wonder to me, since I have seen innumerable testimonies of his Godhead and mission; and I cannot help asking why was not that which I perceive so clearly shown to those people. I have seen man created by God, Eve taken from his side and bestowed upon him as a wife, and both fallen from their first innocence. I have seen the Promise of the messiah, the dispersion of humankind, the wonderful providence of God and His Mysteries preparing the way for the coming of the Blessed Virgin. I saw the descent of the Blessing from which the Word became Flesh running like a path of light through all the generations of Mary's ancestors. At last I saw the angel's message to Mary and the ray of light from the Godhead that penetrated her at the instant the Savior became man.

And after all this, how wonderful did it not seem to me, a miserable, unworthy sinner, to see those holy contemporaries and friends of Jesus in his presence and, though loving and honoring him, yet possessed by the thought that his kingdom was to be an earthly one; to see them regarding him, indeed, as the promised messiah, and yet never dreaming that he was God Himself. He was to them only the son of Joseph and Mary, his mother. None guessed that Mary was a Virgin, for they knew not of her super-

---

[1] Here again a further passage from the notes, for the same reasons given above: "Jesus arose not from Joseph, but—according to the flesh—from Mary alone. But she herself came forth from that holy, prelapsarian Germ which, through the Blessing of Noah, Abraham, etc., became the Blessing in the Ark of the Covenant. And through all this was the Blessing received finally by Joachim and Anne beneath the golden gate of the Temple."

natural immaculate conception; indeed, they knew not even of the Mystery of the Ark of the Covenant.

The Promise and the Place of Baptism

THE place at which John the Baptist taught was about a short hour further on from where he was accustomed to baptize. It was one of the holy memorial places of the Jews and was surrounded by walls like a garden, inside and around which were rush-covered huts. In the center of this enclosure lay a stone upon the spot where the children of Israel, when crossing the Jordan, had first rested the Ark of the Covenant and celebrated a festival of thanksgiving. John had erected his tent for teaching—a large canopy of latticework covered with rushes—over this stone, at whose base was the chair from which he taught. Here John was holding forth to his disciples when Herod came marching by, but he continued his discourse undisturbed by his presence.

John delivered to his disciples at the Jordan a discourse upon the nearness of the messiah's baptism. He told them that he had never seen him, "But," said he, "I shall, as a proof of what I say, show unto you the place at which he will receive baptism. Behold, the waters of the Jordan will divide and from their midst an island will arise." At the same moment I beheld the waters of the river dividing, and on a level with its surface appeared a small, white island circular in shape. This happened at the spot over which the children of Israel had crossed the Jordan with the Ark of the Covenant, and at which also Elijah had divided the waters with his mantle.

The new island, the spot upon which the Ark at the passage through the Jordan rested, appeared to be rocky, and the bed of the river deeper than in Joshua's time. But when John called it forth for the place of Jesus's baptism, the water seemed to be much lower, so that I could not determine whether it had sunk, or the island had risen. I saw that the Jordan was very much swollen when Joshua led the Israelites through it. The Ark of the Covenant was borne far ahead of the people. Among the twelve carriers and attendants were Joshua, Caleb, and one whose name sounded something like Enoi. When they arrived at the Jordan, the forepart of the Ark, which was usually borne by two, was now taken charge of by one alone, while the others supported the back. As soon as the leader set the foot of the Ark in the river, the rushing waters instantly stood still, rose up like galleries on either side, and continued rising and swelling until, like a mountain, they could be seen far away in the region of the city of Zarthan. They flowed toward the Dead Sea, leaving the bed of the river such that the carriers bore the Ark over dry-shod. The Israelites crossed in the same way, but at some distance from the Ark and further down the river. The Ark of the Covenant was borne by the Levites far into the riverbed to a spot upon which were four square, blood-red stones arranged in order. On either side lay two rows of triangular stones, six in number. They were smooth, as if cut with a chisel. Besides these there were twelve others on each side. The twelve Levites set down the Ark of the Covenant on the four central stones and stepped, six to the right, six to the left, on the twelve lying near. These latter were triangular, the sharp end sunk in the earth.

There were twelve others still further off. They too were triangular, very large and massive, and were differently variegated, some of them marked with all kinds of figures and flowers. Joshua caused twelve men from the twelve tribes to be chosen to bear these stones on their shoulders to the shore, and thence to a place at some distance, where they were deposited in a double row for a memorial. At a later period a city rose in the neighborhood of this spot. The names of the twelve tribes and of those that bore them were engraved on the stones. Those upon which the Levites stood were still larger than the others and, before the Israelites left the bed of the river, they were turned so that their point stood upward. The stones borne to the shore were no longer to be seen in John's time. Whether they lay buried in the earth or had been destroyed by war, I cannot now say. John, however, had pitched his tent between the

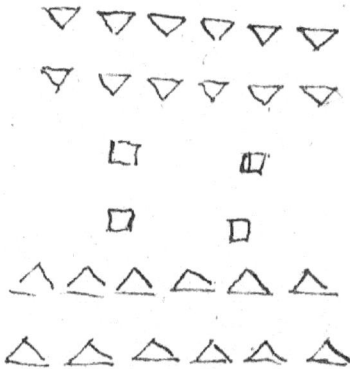

153

sites of the double rows. At a subsequent period, I think through the influence of Helena, a church was built on the spot.

The place upon which the Ark of the Covenant rested in the Jordan was the *exact spot* upon which later on was the baptismal well of Jesus on the island, which otherwise appeared to be destitute of water. When the Israelites and the Ark of the Covenant had crossed and the twelve stones had been turned upward, the Jordan began again to flow.

The Ark, the Promise, and the Baptism in the Jordan

WHEN the voice of God came over Jesus, he was standing alone and in prayer upon the stone. There came from heaven a great, rushing wind like thunder. All trembled and looked up. A cloud of white light descended, and I saw over Jesus a Winged Figure of Light as if flowing over him like a stream. The heavens opened. I beheld an apparition of the heavenly Father in the figure in which he is usually depicted and, in a voice of thunder, heard the words: "This is my beloved Son, in whom I am well pleased." Jesus was perfectly transparent, entirely penetrated by light; one could scarcely look at him. I saw angels around him.

But off at some distance on the waters of the Jordan I saw satan, a dark figure as if in a cloud, and myriads of horrible black reptiles and vermin swarming around him. It was as if all the wickedness, all the sins, all the poison of the whole region took a visible form at the outpouring of the Holy Spirit, and fled into that dark figure as into their original source. The sight was abominable, but it served to heighten the effect of the indescribable splendor and joy and brilliancy spread over the Lord and the whole island. The sacred baptismal well sparkled and glanced—foundations and margin and waters, all a pool of living light. One could see the four stones that had once supported the Ark of the Covenant shining beneath the waters as if in exultation. And on the twelve around the well—those upon which the Levites had stood—appeared angels bending in adoration, for the Spirit of God had before all humankind rendered testimony to the living foundation, to the precious, chosen cornerstone of the Church, around whom we as so many living stones must build up a spiritual edifice, a holy priesthood, that thereby we may offer an acceptable, spiritual sacrifice to God through his beloved Son in whom He is well pleased.

Jesus then ascended the steps and entered the tent near the baptismal well. Saturnin brought the garments, which Lazarus had been holding all this time, and Jesus put them on. When clothed, he left the tent and, surrounded by his disciples, took his stand on the open space near the central tree. John, in joyous tones, addressed the crowd and bore witness to Jesus that he was the Son of God and the promised messiah. He cited the prophecies of the patriarchs and prophets now fulfilled, recounted what he had seen, reminded them of the voice of God which they had heard, and informed them that when Jesus returned he himself would retire. John referred also to the sacred memories that graced the spot upon which they were standing on account of the Ark of the Covenant's having rested here when Israel was journeying to the land of promise. Now, he continued, had they seen the realization of the Covenant witnessed to by his Father, the almighty God Himself. John referred all to Jesus, and called this day, that had beheld the fulfillment of the desire of Israel, blessed.

✝ ✝ ✝ ✝ ✝

ON Sunday, September 25, AD 29, Jesus proceeded to a city named Luz and, going into the synagogue, held a long discourse during which he explained very many ancient mysterious symbols from the scriptures. I remember that he spoke of the children of Israel. After crossing the Red Sea, they had on account of their sins wandered so long in the desert, before being allowed to pass through the Jordan and into the promised land. Now was the actual fulfillment of what was then only typical—for the Baptism in the Jordan had been symbolized by the earlier passage of the Israelites through its waters. If they now remained true and observed God's commands, they should indeed be put into possession of the promised land and the City of God. Jesus spoke in a spiritual sense, signifying thereby the heavenly Jerusalem. But his hearers dreamed only of an earthly kingdom and of deliverance from the Romans. Jesus then spoke of the Ark of the Covenant and of the severity of the old law, for whoever approached so near the Ark as to touch it instantly fell dead; but now was the law fulfilled and grace poured forth in the Son of Man.

On Sunday, January 15, AD 30, while Andrew and Saturnin were baptizing, Jesus gave instruction to the people who had come to the place of baptism. Many had been sent by John, who was now at the second place of baptism, on the east side of the Jordan. John had stopped baptizing and now only preached, speaking always of Jesus. That the spot upon which Jesus had been baptized was the same as that upon which the Ark of the Covenant had stood, and that the stones in the baptismal pool were those upon which it had rested in the bed of the Jordan, were facts known only to Jesus and John, and of which neither had spoken. So too the Lord was the only one who knew that these stones now formed the foundation of the baptismal basin. The Jews had long forgotten the resting place of these stones, and it was not made known to the disciples.

On Tuesday, September 26, AD 30, for the feast of Atonement, Jesus taught in the synagogue regarding penance. He spoke against those who practiced only bodily purification and did not restrain those desires of the soul that were evil. I saw too the celebration of the feast of Atonement in Jerusalem and the numerous purifications of the high priest. The holy Mystery was no longer in the Ark of the Covenant. There were in it only some little linen napkins and the various compartments. This Ark of the Covenant was new and quite different in form from the first. The angels were different. They were seated and surrounded by a triple scarf; one foot was raised, the other hung at the side of the Ark, and the crown was still between them. There were all kinds of sacred things in the Ark, such as oil and incense. I remember that the high priest burned incense and sprinkled blood, that he took one of the little linen cloths from the Ark, that he mixed some blood (which he either drew from his finger or had on his finger) with water, and then presented it to a row of priests to drink. It was a kind of figure of holy communion.

On Sunday, August 31, AD 32, Jesus spoke in Sichar with a couple who wanted to marry. He told them that their plan to marry was motivated by the desire for property. They were shocked that he could read their thoughts, for they had not spoken with anyone about their secret intentions. Then they gave up their plans and believed in Jesus. The people of this region must have had, through their ancestors, some special relations with the Ark of the Covenant. They asked Jesus what had become of the holy Mystery contained in the Ark. He answered that humankind had received so much of it, that it had now passed into them, and that from the fact that it was no longer to be found, they might conclude that the messiah was born. Many people of this country believed that the messiah was put to death among the holy innocents.

About eight months later, on Monday evening (after Easter Sunday), April 6, AD 33, Jesus explained to the apostles several points of holy scripture relative to himself and the blessed sacrament, and ordered the latter to be venerated at the close of the sabbath solemnities. He spoke of the sacred mystery of the Ark of the Covenant; of the bones and relics of ancestors and their veneration—thus to obtain their intercession; of Abraham, and of the bones of Adam that he had had in his possession and that he had laid on the altar when offering sacrifice. Another point relating to Melchizedek's sacrifice, which I then saw, I have forgotten, although it was very remarkable. Jesus further said that the many-colored coat that Jacob gave to Joseph was an emblem of his own bloody sweat on the Mount of Olives.[1]

Jesus likewise told the disciples that Adam's bones—which had been preserved in the Ark of the Covenant—Jacob gave to Joseph along with the many-colored coat. I saw then that Jacob gave them to Joseph without the latter's knowing what they were. Jacob's love prompted him to bestow them upon Joseph as a means of protection, as a treasure, because he knew that his brothers did not love him. Joseph carried the bones hanging on his

---

[1] "At these words I saw that coat of many colors. It was white with broad red stripes. It had three black cords on the breast, with a yellow ornament in the middle. It was full around the body, so that things could be put into it as into a kind of pocket, and girded at the waist. It was narrow below and had slits at the side to afford more room for walking. It reached to the ankles, was longer behind than before, and on the breast was open down to the girdle. Joseph's ordinary dress reached only to the knee."

breast in a little pouch formed of two leathern tablets, not square, but rounded on top. When his brothers sold him, they took from him only the colored coat and the undergarment, leaving him a bandage around his loins and a scapular on his breast. It was under the latter that the little pouch hung. On going into Egypt, Jacob questioned Joseph about that treasure and revealed to him that it was Adam's bones. Again I saw the bones under Mount Golgotha. They were white as snow and still very hard. Some of Joseph's own bones were preserved in the Ark of the Covenant.

Jesus spoke too of the Mystery contained in the Ark of the Covenant. He said that that Mystery was now his body and blood, which he gave to them forever in the sacrament. He spoke of his own passion and of some wonderful things relating to David, of which they were ignorant and which he explained. Lastly, he bade them go in a couple of days to the region of Sichar, and there proclaim his resurrection. After that he vanished. I saw the apostles and disciples going around among one another, perfectly intoxicated with joy. They opened the doors, went in and out, and assembled again under the lamp, to sing canticles of praise and thanksgiving.

www.ingramcontent.com/pod-product-compliance
Lightning Source LLC
Chambersburg PA
CBHW022008080426
42733CB00007B/523